Social Relevance
of
Higher Learning Institutions

About the Author

Prof. G. Palanithurai, Rajiv Gandhi Chair for Panchayati Raj Studies, Gandhigram Rural University, India, is an academic activist. He is specialized in Grassroots Democracy, Decentralized Governance and Development Management. His action research activities are supported by the Ford Foundation, Swiss Development and Cooperation, The Hunger Project, Population Foundation of India, DANIDA, Action Aid International, Ministry of Panchayati Raj, Ministry of Rural Development, Government of India, Toolkit Foundation, Netherlands, UNDP, State Planning Commission and a few other agencies in India and abroad. He has developed a leadership school in Rajiv Gandhi Chair for Panchayati Raj Studies.

He has worked for the preparation of 10th and 11th Five Year Plans for Tamil Nadu through State Planning Commission. He worked for the 1st, 2nd, and 3rd State Finance Commissions and for which he conducted a number of studies related to panchayat finance. He has published 63 books, 139 articles in refereed jounals, 83 monographs, 76 popular articles in his area of specialization in popular dailies. He has availed the fellowship from Shastri Indo-Canadian Institute twice, World Academy of Art and Science, USA, Toolkit Foundation, Netherlands, to conduct studies and write books. He has visited the US, Canada, Singapore, Sri Lanka, Senegal and Malaysia on academic assignments. He has introduced two innovative M.A. Programmes, one in Development Management and another in Governance and Development are supported by University Grants Commission, New Delhi. He has organized 2 International programmes, 15 National programmes and 61 Regional programmes with the financial support of various agencies. He made presentations in 20 international conferences, 145 national programmes and 67 regional seminars and conferences. He prepared two District Human Development Reports for Dindigul and Nagapattinam Districts.

Social Relevance of Higher Learning Institutions

G. Palanithurai

CONCEPT PUBLISHING COMPANY Pvt. Ltd,
NEW DELHI-110059

ISBN-13: 978-81-8069-863-7

First Published 2012

Published and Printed by

Concept Since 1974

Concept Publishing Company Pvt. Ltd.
A/15-16, Commercial Block, Mohan Garden
New Delhi-110059 (India)
T: 25351460, 25351794, *F*: 091-11-25357109
E: publishing@conceptpub.com, W: www.conceptpub.com
Editorial Office: H-13, Bali Nagar, New Delhi-110 015, India.

Cataloging in Publication Data DK–*Courtesy:* D.K. Agencies (P) Ltd. <docinfo@dkagencies.com>

Palanithurai, G. (Ganapathy)
Social relevance of higher learning institutions / G. Palanithurai.
p. cm.
Includes bibliographical references (p.) and index.
ISBN 9788180698637

1. Education, Higher—Social aspects—India. 2. Education, Rural—India. 3. University extension—India. I. Title.

DDC 378.54 23

Acknowledgements

I never claim that I am an expert in Higher Education. In India it is undergoing a radical change both in structure and form in the recent decades and as a result it receives severe criticism from the experts on education and opinion makers. In the past higher education was criticized on the poor quality and quantity, non-responsiveness of the academics and poor infrastructural facilities. Of late it is being attacked by different stakeholders as it takes business character without any principle. It is being rocked because of the corrupt practices developed and adopted in higher education in every process from top to bottom. As a result it has lost its moral stature. At this point of time I started expressing my opinion in many fora and subsequently I have involved in writing popular and research articles on higher education. But I claim that I am an academic activist. I work in a Gandhian Institution with a focus of reaching out to the society directly through our outreach programmes. Being fed up with the conventional university I have joined in an unconventional university when I got an opportunity. Till I joined in Gandhigram I thought that teaching and research were the primary functions of the University teachers. After joining in Gandhigram I began to learn that there is another dimension in higher education, namely outreach programme. After learning extension I came to realize the full potentials of higher learning institutions. I have been working in all the domains very creatively for the past twenty years in a Gandhian Institution. I never confined myself only in teaching. I have been teaching, doing research and carrying out outreach programmes in the areas of my specialization. I looked at higher education in India from three dimensions such as teaching, research and extension. What I found in higher education in India is totally an incomplete education in form as the three components of education, namely teaching, research and outreach activities, are not carried out in an integrated way. If the higher education is active and vibrant in all the three aspects, many of the problems in the society could be tackled very easily. But the reality in higher education is that it remains only in teaching and partially in research. Further higher education has been commercialized and the quality has gone down beyond imagination. I have started analyzing the reasons for the sudden decline and deterioration of higher education while it is being expanded and I have started writing about it. As a result slowly I have moved over to the management and governance of the higher learning institutions. I have written articles on the functioning of the higher learning institutions. They are published in different journals and mostly in university news. After the publication of the articles I got letters from the editors of some of the journals asking for articles. Further I got letters from many criticizing my articles. A few encouraged me to write more such articles as my articles have focused on accountability issues of academic institutions. The criticisms and appreciations have prompted me to write further. Having done eight articles published in different journals my colleagues requested me to compile the articles into a small monograph. Though I have focused more on accountability I have been touching on the missing dimension of our education system, outreach or extension programme. I have been indicating the potentials available in the higher learning institutions to the teachers connect themselves with society for the benefits of the communities and for themselves.

Gandhigram Rural Institute, Deemed University, has provided me an opportunity to conduct series of experiments in higher education and for which I must pay my homage to the founder of the Institute Dr. G. Ramachandran a great Gandhian educationalist who laid the strong foundation for extension oriented Rural Institute in Gandhigram. Since he was a student of Tagore and a co-worker of Mahatma Gandhi, his vision of rural higher education was sound. I have picked up the main thread for my arguments only from the writings of Dr. G Ramachandran. Secondly, all the Vice-Chancellors of Gandhigram Rural Institute enabled me to do such creative and innovative experiments in the Gandhigram Rural Institute in teaching, research and outreach programmes. There might have been setbacks and failures. Yet some of the activities are very useful to the society and stakeholders. All our activities are supported by various funding agencies apart from University Grants Commission. I have to recognize many donor agencies who liberally funded all our research and outreach activities and hence, I must thank them profusely. Based on my experiments I have written articles about the status of higher learning institutions in India. The articles which I have written are critical account of higher learning institutions. I always take a position that one has to critically examine whether we have performed our task, roles and responsibilities before criticizing others. Against this background I have written articles and I have indicated the potentials and they are not being used. Along with the above articles I have added three more articles in the volume written in Germany based on my experience. I was in Germany for six months (one full semester) serving Cologne University as Visiting (Guest) Professor. Having taught the students in a different academic environment I was tempted to write my experience. Hence, I have written an article. My staff both teaching and project enabled me to devote my time fully to do such innovative works in evolving new academic, research and outreach programmes. They all cooperated with me and actively participated in the whole process along with me. All the teaching staff and non-teaching staff are highly cooperative and facilitative. In equal measure my family members allowed me to do my work without demanding my time for their work. Hence, I register my thanks to my staff in the Department and my family members in my house for their active cooperation and encouragement throughout my academic journey.

G. PALANITHURAI

Contents

List of Tables

List of Diagrams

Introduction

Higher education in India is all time low at present in terms of its quality and the functioning of the higher learning institutions is in shambles. Always higher education in India was and is far away from the poor as very limited seats were available in public institutions and now abundant seats are available but they are not unaffordable to the poor. As a result poor could not go nearer to higher education. If the poor are able to reach the institutions the quality of education which they get is poor. Now higher education is in market mode but market theory of supply and demand does not work. Adam Smith's role of invisible hand is absent in this market system. It is a peculiar market. It helps only the rich and helps educational businessmen and women. Seats are more in number but the cost of the seats is also very high as all regulatory authorities have lost their control over the institutions. It is a new economics we find in Indian higher education. Businessmen and politicians have moved over to educational business not to serve but to make profit. Thirty years back the cost of higher education was very cheap but the value of the degree was very high. Based on the grade and capability of the certificate holder jobs were offered. Now the cost of education is very high but the value of the degree is very less. Jobs are offered not on the basis of the skill and capacity but on the capability of the candidate to pay for the job. When jobs were offered on the basis of skill and capability, assigned duties were performed and salaries were given moderately. Now salary is very high and hence to fetch a job one has to pay. But the assigned duties needed not be performed and nobody will ensure such accountability. Jobs with high end salary are available for capacitated and skilled candidates. Those jobs are being offered not on the basis of certificates and grades but on the basis of the proven skills of the candidates. Thus higher education system is in paradoxical situation. On the one hand higher educational institutions are expanded and produced manpower to the market. It is to be noted that only a select set of institutions belonging to public and private sectors have produced quality manpower needed to the market. There is another set of institutions belonging to public and private sectors have produced manpower without needed skill and capacity needed to the market. In such a way system of higher education is developed.

To steamline higher education there are many regulatory and supervisory authorities like All India Medical Council, All India Technical Education Council, Teacher Education Council and the UGC. Everyone knows in the country how the chairpersons and secretaries of those councils were arrested and suspended. Many of the houses of such authorities were raided by the CBI search teams on suspicion and allegation. Vice-Chancellors have been suspended and many have got anticipatory bails. Inquiry Committees were constituted to conduct inquiry on the allegations made by many on the Vice-Chancellors and Directors of the institutions. Totally the moral authority of the regulatory institutions has been dismantled. Rates have been fixed for the position of the Vice-Chancellors. As a result visionaries, scholars and committed academics are keeping themselves away from the corridors of power. Academic giants are in the universities as professors and dwarfs are in the helm of affairs. This is the condition of the public institutions barring a few. Vice-Chancellors are supposed to be the leaders giving leadership to the institutions and image builders of the universities. They are the visionaries of the institutions. They will stand more on moral authority. Their moral stature is very high. Now they become brokers, managers and sometimes dealers in higher learning institutions. As a result they are not in a position to provide vision leadership and direction. The Vice-Chancellors are engaged in routine activities of signing the papers processed by the clerks. But somehow or the other they are in the process of managing the resources what they have given to get these positions.

Everyone knows how Vice-Chancellors are being appointed. It is being discussed openly in the media. There are news items in the media that Vice-Chancellors have made statements that they have given money and they are to be taken. When remarks are made about such a kind of appointments in the media, nobody from the Government took cognizance and refuted the charge. Media observations are not contested. Neither the political party leaders nor the opinion-makers have shown concern to this sorry state of affairs in higher education in

India. At least intellectuals could have played their role properly to get rid of the maladies. Academicians who are in the universities could have raised questions to arrest the deterioration of the higher learning institutions. They have also done nothing as they are not being touched by the Vice-Chancellors. The Vice-Chancellors are busy in their work either in managing himself to mobilize the money given for the position and to get some other positions after his tenure as Vice-Chancellor. Hence, they do not want to antagonize the teachers and the non-teaching staff. The students were once organized for public cause. Now they are not being organized by the political parties. Hence, it is a safe zone for money making business for everyone. Individually everyone is safe but collectively they are in danger zone. It is a tragedy of a public case. As one finds caste hierarchy in the society, institutions are of different standards. We have in our country that 'A' class institution to 'F' class institutions. 'A' class institutions are meant for rich business class, political class, bureaucratic class and other middle class families. They can afford to pay any amount of money as one pays in the US. Other classes of institutions are meant for other classes of the society. Poor can go to 'F' class where adequate facilities are not available and it is dead cheap compared to 'A' class. The 'F' class institutions give admission to the poor students free of cost. Because nothing is there in these institutions except the poor classrooms and teachers without commitment. But the certificates issued by the 'F' class institutions are neither valued by the employers nor the people who are holding the certificates. This graded higher education has increased the number of unemployables. But it helped the government to project the higher rate of enrolment in higher learning institutions. On the other hand it adds problems as unemployment rate is increased and on the other hand it increased the enrolment rate. It never helped the society and industry by producing needed quality manpower. At present the Indian society needs more manpower to meet the market requirements. To meet the requirements educational institutions have been expanded and increased with the active participation of the private sector. The private sector which entered into the education business is not the private as we are seeing in the West. We have seen the contributions of the charity houses in higher education in the past. But the new charity houses are not in charity but in making money. By seeing the green pastures they have entered into the new domain with the basic objective of making maximum profit in the shortest period of time. From the above background one can imagine what kind of educational ambience would be created by these new private sectors? Barring a few many of the higher learning institutions have neither vision nor mission for their institutions. They have created institutions by violating all institutional and regulatory norms through corrupt means. Their entry into higher education has provided enormous opportunities to the bureaucrats and the politicians to make money. It is a new business. Yet one set of institutions apart from the premier institutions of India have contributed substantially the needed manpower to the market. Yet market needs could not be met as a section of the private sector could not produce the quality manpower needed to the market.

What is the way out for this existing mess in higher education? is the basic question. Answer lies elsewhere. Now 'education' as a subject in the concurrent list and as a result nobody owns responsibility. Everybody has contributed for the existing conditions of higher learning instituions. Where to start the correction is yet another question. Arguments and counter arguments are on to find solutions. In this process I have also written articles and published the same in different journals. But my point of view is not only criticism but I looked at the issues from the perspectives of solutions that too from teachers who are in higher education institutions. How the committed teachers in higher educational institutions can play an effective role in arresting the fall of the standard of higher education in India and it is being explored and explained in my articles. Before accusing the other stakeholders for the present state of deterioration, teachers have to critically examine whether they have performed the roles and responsibilities effectively and efficiently to the level of expectation and commensurate to the emoluments they get from the public purse. A teacher has to perform three roles in higher educational institutions, namely—teaching, research and extension. They are to be performed integrally and meaningfully. The proportion may vary from individual to individual depending on the need and the facilities and opportunities available in the institutions. One can concentrate more on teaching, less on research and outreach and *vice versa*. Yet for meaningful teaching both research and extensions are imperative and *vice versa*. Many of the ills in society, politics, economics, governance and administration are due to the failure of the knowledge institutions, namely higher learning institutions or the universities. Many of the challenges of the society, governance, economics and politics are unattended to by the knowledge institutions in India. I have written a little on the above subjects. They are published in different journals in different periods. They are being edited for this book. All the articles are arranged in this book in two parts. Part one consists of five articles. Part two consists of three articles. Part one deals with higher education system and its weaknesses and they have been captured in these articles. First article entitled "Where We Lead in Higher Education?" explains the contextual crises in higher education system in India. The issues are analyzed contextually and the reasons for this crisis are explained. Second article briefly analyses the reasons for lowering of quality in higher education and how every stakeholder contributed for lowering the quality of higher education in India. Third article "System and Stakeholder in Higher Education" argues the role of the stakeholders in correcting the maladies in higher education at present. This article succinctly argues that how teachers can effectively perform their roles and intervene in the corrective process of higher education. Fourth article entitled "Larger Role of Academics in Rural Human Life" explains the potentials available in the higher education system to extend to the society directly. Rural life can be improved a lot with the active intervention of the academics of higher educational institutions. This paper argues very effectively the role could be played by higher educational institutions through outreach programmes of universities and colleges. Article Five of Part One brings to light the experience the author had in Canada while interacting with the researchers of Park Land Institute of Alberta University. The author compared with the experience he had in Rajiv Gandhi Chair for Panchayati Raj Studies in Gandhigram Rural Institute. By doing so the author brings an argument that a teacher can do enormous amount of activities apart from teaching if he or she has got commitment to serve the society by using the institutions. It is a mere narration of his own personal experience in carrying out research and outreach programmes. He powerfully brings an argument that teachers have a major role in social transformation. In article six "Role of Teachers in Higher Education System" the author brought the basic qualities and duties of a leader in higher learning institutions. Seventh article brings out the characters of a model or an ideal department in a university system. The author in the eighth article entitled "Education System of Germany: Special Focus on Higher Education" highlighted the basic features of the education system of Germany. This article was based on his personal experience as he served as visiting professor (Guest) in the Centre for Modern Indian Studies, Cologne University, Germany for one semester. This article is incorporated in this book for the purpose of comparison.

Part two speaks about the role to be performed by the higher educational institutions in the form of extension. Academic institutions have to teach, to do research and to carry out outreach programmes in the communities through extension more intensively. The author has continuously pointed out the missing dimension 'Extension' in the higher education system. His firm conviction is that many of the ills in the communities can easily be tackled if the higher educational institutions are connected themselves with the society directly through meaningful outreach programmes. Article nine of the section two brought to light the role of the universities and colleges in tackling the issues of the communities which emanate from the impact of Globalization. What exact roles can be performed by the universities in the era of globalization is explained succinctly in this article? Article ten indicated the lapse on the part of the higher education system by doing an important role 'extension' systematically through institutional arrangements. He suggested in this article ways and means to incorporate the scheme of extension in the education programme of higher educational institutions.

Article eleven entitled "Reinventing and Contextualizing the Rural Universities" brought to light a new dimension in the Indian higher education system "Rural University System" in India. It came from Gandhian School of Thought. Many experiments had been conducted on this line. Yet there is no evidence to prove that it is the most suitable system for India. However, it is also in vogue. Potentials are explained but not achieved. Hence, based on the limited experience of the author, being a part in those experiments traced the origin, growth and development of the system and explained the problems associated with the successful running of the system. In this article the author has contextualized the rural university system to meet the requirement of the rural society in the era of globalization.

On the whole, this book covers certain major issues of higher education system in India. While covering some of the issues author's focus was on the missing dimension of the higher education system "Extension". By doing so he has contextualized the roles to be performed by the universities in the communities in the form of outreach activities. He has indicated the available and unused potentials in the higher education system in the form of extendable. He has shown the possibilities to perform the roles through his own personal experiences.

Moreover, he has focused his attention on the rural university system and its relevance in this work. Being a part in the rural university system he has extensively analyzed its genesis growth and development of the rural university system in India. He also indicated the scope for repositioning rural university system in India in the context of globalization.

Part I

Higher Education in India

1
Where We Lead in Higher Education

Introduction

India is known for several paradoxes of which one is the way her higher education institutions are responding to the challenges of the twenty first century created by the globalisation of the economy and making use of the opportunities to achieve prosperity and contribute to a knowledge economy[1]. To make use of the new opportunities the higher education institutions have to adapt fast to the emerging trends[2]. In the process of making use of the opportunities, threats have affected and afflicted the higher education system, ultimately creating a crisis in India. Originally the higher education system was created with the objective of creating knowledge and disseminating the same for the purpose of helping society to move to higher level activities[3]. But now the higher education system has been reduced to producing students as marketable products instead creating ethical, informed and enlightened citizens. Students now enter the higher education institutions by paying huge amounts as fees and emerge with the mindset that they have to get back the money which they have invested in this education. As a result the economic principle of demand and supply works in the higher education system too. Ultimately the issues which have affected all other sectors have affected the education sector also.

To address the issues and the problems in higher education, steps have been taken by the Central Government by appointing committees and by organizing conferences, workshops and consultations. The committees and conferences have prepared reports[4] which have ultimately created confusion as to which direction and with what approach and perspective we are going to move in higher education in India. From the reports one can easily identify the contradiction between the Government and the University Grants Commission. No doubt the reports have brought out the issues afflicting the system and suggested remedial measures. But the reports have also produced contradictions between schools of thought in the government itself and among the scholars involved in preparing the reports and among the institutions involved in policy making[5]. The present write up tries to underline the current crisis in higher education and suggest ways and means to evolve a framework to regulate higher education in India.

Context

Globalisation has created unprecedented opportunity in the economy and the same can be exploited only by creating needed manpower. The condition of the higher education system in India is one of needs for more partners to invest in higher education so that the needed manpower can be created for the market. The governments cannot find adequate resources for investment in immediate expansion in higher education. As a result, it has no other option but to allow private players in the higher education system. India has got a tradition of private players in the higher education system. But, now, it has become a business venture. Previously, from the days of the British, private players came forward as their social responsibility to support the government and the society to increase the enrolment of students in higher education. But now the context prompts the private players to take up roles in higher education not as corporate social responsibility but purely as a business venture to make profit and more profit by making use of the new opportunities to prepare manpower for global demands[6]. Even if it is a business, it can provide quality manpower suitable to the market. But it is not done and this ultimately creates the current problem.

Since education is in the concurrent list, both the Central and the State Governments could have developed a framework through which the new institutions could have been regulated systematically to function as partners of government to produce manpower. Unfortunately the old system of screening continues to function and thereby the new institutions were screened and they were allowed to play their role. All the institutions were thoroughly examined as per the existing norms and, on the basis of the recommendations, deemed universities status was given. Justification was given by the Chairman of UGC[7]. This opening of creating deemed universities was thought of because of the existing rigid system of higher education. Hence, everyone moved through the deemed university route. Originally deemed university status was conferred for uniqueness or for specialization. It is normal that any sudden expansion needs a new institutional mechanism and, in the absence of the new, the old one has to be equipped to meet the requirements. In India there was no new institutional set up nor any expansion of the existing mechanism to cope with the increased opportunity. As a result corruption crept into the system. The whole higher education system is choked by corruption and has not delivered the goods needed to the economy, and as a result, people are exploited and it has added to the unemployment problem rather than solving the problem[8]. For all the ills afflicting the higher education system, the poor performance of the regulatory mechanism which supervised the functioning of the higher education institutions is responsible[9]. Liberalization has been used to liberate the whole process of supervision by dubious means and thereby private business groups have entered into the education market. As a result now we find in the education market one set of high class institutions with all facilities and qualified staff performing the task of producing the manpower needed for the economy. This set of institutions has helped the cream of the society. Entry is highly restricted to the elites. Yet another set of institutions has been created with inadequate facilities and poor quality of the staff. They also lure the aspirants and send them as products to the market. But they cannot be absorbed in the market. As a result we find a crisis of unemployment. Here it is to be noted that one cannot ignore the role played by the private players in higher education in enrolment of students[10]. Of the institution both government aided and managed and private managed, which segment creates problems and what are the problems they create, are to be analyzed in an integrated way. In all sectors we find problems while opening the avenues for private. We have taken decisions to tackle all those problems. In the same way we try to find out suitable ways and means to correct them. But a word of caution that education sector connoted be treated like telecom or power or transport sector. To understand the whole problem, primarily we have to analyze the issue contextually, institutionally, managerially and functionally.

Classification of Institutions

In India we have multiplicity of institutions. The first set of institutions are funded by the government and they are adequately equipped and cater to the needs of the competently equipped students. They are IITs, IIMs, IISs and nationally recognized institutions. They produce quality products on a limited scale but not to the requirements of the market in terms of quantity. These institutions have not grown physically to produce the needed quantity of manpower for the market. There is another set of public institutions which cater to all segments of the society. The facilities are moderate and the staffs are qualified but not up-to-date. These institutions have performed moderately in producing quality products. These sets of institutions are facing paucity of funds. Contextual change has not been effected in their programmes. They are the state universities and government colleges. Absolutely accountability is weak and it is a free ride for politicians through government. The third set of institutions were started long back with the assistance of government grants but under private management. The programmes are updated periodically and accountability is maintained despite inadequate facilities. Some of the institutions have changed their programmes periodically as they have got autonomy from the university system. They are government aided private colleges.

A further set of institutions is totally new. They are of two types. One is those started with commercial interest on a permanent basis. These institutions are well equipped and well established. The above institutions are professionally maintained to meet the market requirements. They are in the market. They are professionally equipped and well maintained and scientifically administered. Another set is purely temporary and driven by profit motive with poor quality of professionals, inadequate facilities with poor staff strength. This set of institutions will function as long as they fetch profit. The moment the market crashes they will quit higher education and move to new businesses just as they came to this sector. Now we hear the news about the sale of colleges and institutions. It is because of the commercial nature of the institutions. Having judged the surging aspirations of the middle class and the poor for higher education and the existing weak and corrupt regulatory mechanism these new institutions have entered into the market. Following are the details of the institutions in the higher education domain.

Table 1.1: Categories of Universities

S. No.	*Type of Universities*		*Number as on 31-5-2009*
1.	Central Universities		40
2.	State Universities		235
3.	Deemed Universities		
	Government	41	
	Private	86	127
4.	National Importance (State)		5
5.	National Importance (Centre)		33
6.	Private Universities		39
	Total		479

Source: University Grants Commission.

Responding to Market Needs

In the context of expanding opportunity, the first two sets of institutions have not expanded to the level of requirement with increased public funding because the government has to invest heavily in primary and secondary education. The third set of institutions have maintained the *status quo* but there is no initiative for expansion of quantity and enhancement of quality. The institutions which have been maintained by private charitable organisations have expanded the scope of intake but not improved the quality.

The first set of institutions have improved themselves and contextualized yet they cannot meet the market requirement of manpower. The second and the third set of institutions have not improved and contextualized their functioning and their programmes of activities. These institutions are functioning under the framework of the bureaucratic system and they enjoy very limited autonomy. Even within the autonomy given to the institutions needed changes could have been effected but unfortunately it was not done as the institutions had poor and weak leadership and there was no social commitment on the part of the academics. The academics do not have professional pride, with a few rare exceptions. Hence they could not respond to the challenges of the new dispensation of globalisation.

The fourth set of institutions have responded to the challenges by creating institutions with needed facilities and professionals. They have performed the production of students in terms of quantity and quality. There is yet another group of institutions in the same fourth set quickly entered into the market with pure business motive produced students in quantity without quality expected from the market. In this category a large number of institutions were started with a profit motive even by selling old business units. All the established norms have been dismantled by these institutions. Both the types of this set of institutions have tried to escape from the ambit of the government regulations by making use of a provision to confer deemed university status and thereby these institutions are made autonomous. They want to escape from the control of the State Governments to increase the intake of students and to collect fees from the students without any question. The conditions are favourable for this move because the first three sets of institutions have been facing a multiplicity of problems which detracted those institutions from repositioning themselves to cope with the new demand from the market for manpower. Academic and research programmes have been introduced as they find market and fees have been fixed arbitrarily and the whole process is a free ride. Many of the institutions do not have required facilities and qualified staff and yet they fix fees at higher levels. Absolutely there is no regulatory mechanism. It is true that even regular State and Central Universities are also not having a regulatory mechanism. At least in the Central and State Universities' executive bodies, government representatives are made members. Moreover the Central and State Universities have fixed fees and intake of students. They cannot violate those norms. They may not be able to produce quality manpower to the required quantity. The problems of the state universities are managerial, administrative, governance, financial and so on. Hence, the fourth set of institutions have utilized the weak points of the first three sets of institutions and entered into the domain as free riders. They have created problems by exploiting the people by setting up the sub-standard institutions and extracting huge amounts of money from the students and producing students of poor quality far below the expected standard of the market.

Remedies

In order to streamline the problem afflicting the higher education institutions, the Government of India has constituted committees and produced vision documents. They are Knowledge Commission report, University Grants Commission report and Yashpal Committee report. All the reports were prepared during the UPA regime. The report of the UGC was prepared through a lengthy process of consultations and stakeholders' participation. The other two reports are good reports but elitist in orientation and approach. It is to be noted here that education is not a central subject or a state subject but is in the concurrent list. But a substantial number of state governments have not taken serious steps like the Federal Government to revamp the system. Instead the state governments have used this opportunity to add confusion and alleged that the Central Government has taken away the power of the states on the subject of education since it is in the concurrent list. All the three reports, though they contradict one another, underline the need for revamping the whole higher education system. The discussions were on governance, management, financing and innovation. The focus is on expansion, inclusion and excellence. This focus is due to the expanding market for more human resource, to include the underprivileged and hitherto excluded into the system and to achieve excellence in higher education. It is a process of competing with other countries in supplying quality manpower to the economy and to make profit through a knowledge economy. Based on the observations and recommendations, steps have been taken to correct the maladies in the system.

Manpower Need

The whole target for expansion is not based on the realistic assessment of the manpower requirement of the world and the country in particular. The very function of higher education institutions is to produce skilled and capable manpower for productive activities in the economy and to create new knowledge. For balanced economy manpower planning is an imperative. The higher education system will play an important role in improving the economy and reducing the social problems, if the supply and demand match. Manpower planning and human resource preparation have to be managed thus. But in India both are not done very scientifically. The moment the private players sensed the gap, they filled in the gap by organizing institutions and the whole process was quick and hence all kinds of problems arose in the higher education system. The poor quality of higher education is due to unregulated institutions and poor quality of human resource production which ultimately exploited the people and caused unemployment problem in the society. A social menace has been created by these institutions. Against this background the remedial steps are on. For this remedial action strong political will is needed as the majority of violators and profit seekers in the higher education system are politicians of the lower order and businessmen of the lower order. Ethical politics and business will not create any such problem as we face today in India. Private players are in higher education system in the West also. They are not facing such problems as we face here. These groups have not only created problems through their institutions but also corrupted the entire political and bureaucratic class and thereby the other three sets of institutions have also been disturbed managerially, administratively and in other modes.

Analysis of the Issues

To overcome the above crisis one has to look at the problems broadly and systematically. The problems cannot be simplified and narrowed down to mere commercialization or privatization of higher education. Further it is to be seen contextually, historically, institutionally and functionally. By doing so, one can locate the problem in the structural, policy, administrative, financial and functional domains. The whole issue started when the higher education domain expanded due to the requirement of manpower due to the increased demand in the market both in India and abroad. So expanding the higher education institutions was an imperative need. Expansion requires huge investment in the higher education sector for which the government did not have adequate resources. Even in the normal course public institutions will not mend or amend according to the contextual change quickly on their own however autonomous they are. The stakeholders in the public institutions tend to think that system maintenance and *status quo* maintenance will be the safer course of action. It is only the market force which will act fast to respond to the challenges and changes of the context. Hence the government allowed the private players to come in.

In the existing arrangement of institutions, namely the first two sets of institutions, there was no possibility to meet the new demand. Hence necessarily private players had to be allowed. In this process two groups of private players entered. One group deliberately planned to stay on in this sector and make their institutions professionally competitive. It appears that their strategy is to put the service in business mode. There is yet another group, purely a commercial venture to exploit the demand at the quickest possible and as long as possible and there is no long term interest. They are racketeers. They do not have any ethics and their entry into the higher education system has destabilized the whole educational management system in India. These groups make profit on the aspirations of the emerging new middle class and the ignorance of the poor. The second type deliberately mobilized huge resources and sometimes closed their earlier ventures by selling their industries and invested in higher education institutions. In the sudden expansion all have moved into the domain by utilizing the weak regulatory mechanism which was already corrupted.

Despite proliferation of institutions and production of students on a massive scale, the market requirements are not met qualitatively. The market requires skilled manpower. But institutions could not produce not even one-third of manpower acceptable to the market. As a result a large chunk returned to the unemployed army and remained unemployable. The reason for the inability of the new institutions to produce quality manpower is basically due to the poor quality of the teachers. The newly created institutions could not find quality staff from the market for the sudden expansion. To attract the students the institutions have used the names of luminaries in the field fictitiously. The products of all the institutions were absorbed in the market as the market was expanding. But the slowdown in the economy naturally ejected a chunk from employment. The ejected were from the bottom of their recruitment. Despite the slowdown of the economy and the ejection of employees from the market, the institutions have not regulated their functioning. They continue to produce their products as unemployables. So a mismatch has emerged between the market demand and the supply of personnel from the higher education institutions.

In the first and second set of higher education institutions, much change was not effected and hence they remained as they were. They could not increase their intake. Hence, for the aspirants and for the market, there was no choice excepting relying on the private players. It is to be noted here that it is only the private institutions that have substantially enrolled students in higher education institutions and substantially produced graduates for the market needs. It is because of the foul players that the higher education system has got mixed up and got into trouble. Simply because of the troubles we face one cannot wish away the role of the private players in the higher education system[11]. So these issues cannot be dealt with as in the telecom sector or other sectors. How to classify the private as good and bad? It can be done only through a rating of the private institutions. Further a minimum standard has to be set through a regulatory mechanism. We have regulatory authorities but in the sudden expansion the regulatory authorities could not expand their activities. The evils of globalisation have affected this sector as they affected the other sectors. As a result the regulatory authorities remained nominal heads rather than becoming effective instruments regulating the higher education institutions. The regulatory authorities have been corrupted. These are natural when sudden expansion takes place in any sector. The whole world is deliberating on new regulatory mechanism for economy after seeing the fall of the market economy[12]. We witness the same in higher education. How to regulate the institutions to perform their task perfectly, professionally and profitably for the advantage of the individuals concerned and the country is now the question.

The new target fixed for enrolment in higher education system in India by comparing other Asian countries and Western countries requires new institutions. When the governments are not able to find resource for expansion, it is a welcome move to involve private players. When private players are coming into this sector in the context of the market economy one cannot expect the same values with which private players started institutions through their charities at the dawn of Independence in India. The old private players had come to serve the society by sacrifice but the new players have come to the higher education sector not with the objective of serving the society *per se* but the new mantra 'Serve and Prosper' quite against the old mantra 'Serve and Sacrifice'. Even with this new mantra "serve and prosper", there is nothing wrong in it if the products coming out of the higher education institutions are getting opportunity in the job market by equipping themselves. So the new mantra is applicable to all.

But the question is whether the newly created private higher education institutions have performed their role professionally to meet the market demand. When we look at the newly created institutions in terms of their performance, the performance of the other set of the institutions starting from the second set has to be evaluated systematically. Because even traditional universities funded by the government, colleges run by private charitable institutions and by the government are deeply affected by a series of problems and as a result they are also producing unemployable substandard graduates. Some of the newly created deemed universities are far better than some of the public funded full-fledged state universities and deemed universities. Hence the mess is in the whole system, not only in the newly created deemed universities. To set right the maladies a comprehensive framework enforced through a well regulated mechanism is needed. Occasional outbursts and arbitrary evaluations and hasty decisions will not solve the problems. Instead they will create more problems. So, a series of steps are needed now to revamp the higher education institutions. Primarily the government institutions and government aided institutions have to be well equipped in terms of facilities and faculty. One cannot presume that the public funded universities and colleges are all having qualified staff. Of course, they are qualified educationally but they are not professionally equipped.

The political interference in the universities and the colleges have effectively prevented the entry of qualified and professionally competitive staff and as a result substandard personnel have entered into the higher education portals as teachers through dubious means. Hence a thorough evaluation is needed for public funded institutions also. The intake capacity has to be doubled after equipping the institutions infrastructurally. Along with this the shift system has to be introduced and then the market demands can be met. Secondly, the private institutions which have got adequate facilities have to be made full-fledged universities. Some of the deemed universities are far better than some of the state universities. Hence their elevation to the level of universities is an imperative. Thirdly, the private institutions which are lagging behind have to be regulated and they should be allowed to take in only a minimum number of students till they equip themselves infrastructurally and human resource-wise. To overcome, all these problems two regulatory authorities have to be created.[13] One is for conduct of examinations and the other one is for collection of fees. For the above two tasks two institutional set-ups have to be created. All institutions, private, public, quasi-public, aided etc. can run programmes for which they will be autonomous but examinations have to be conducted by an independent agency.

By doing so in the competitive process the weak institutions will fade away from the market as the market mechanism will work.

Secondly, the fees for programmes have to be collected only by an independent agency which has to collect the fees and remit the same to the institutions based on the number of students admitted. By effecting this regulation the present exploitation of the people can be avoided and standards can be maintained through the common examination system. Instead of creating chaos and confusion with a careful selection from a battery of solutions the higher education system can be revamped and saved from deep malaise and the same can be made powerful engine to produce professionals for the market rather than producing students to join the unemployed army.

Conclusion

The existing problems in the higher education system are many of which exploiting of the people by the institutions and production of poor quality of manpower are the most important and serious. Setting up of an appropriate higher educations system, evolving of a new higher education policy, creation of an appropriate regulating mechanism and allocation of adequate resources are very essential at present. Further it is not merely the evaluation of the deemed universities alone that is needed. A comprehensive analysis of all sets of institutions is an imperative. The existing regulatory mechanism has to be made more rigorous and transparent. While evaluating the performance of the institutions, the outcome should be the indicator and not the output. While evolving an evaluative framework, multiple frameworks have to be evolved to suit the requirements of the institutions based on different sets of objectives. Further an independent agency for fees collection and examination system will eliminate many of the evils which have crept into the higher education system.

Notes and References

1. J. Salmi, *Tertiary Education in the 21st century: Challenges and Opportunities,* Washington DC: World Bank, 2000.
2. Anthony Stella and A. Gnanam, *Looking Ahead: A Decade of Accreditation in Retrospect: Development in Quality Assurance of Higher Education in India,* Bangalore: Aicra Publishers, 2004.

3. International Commission on Peace and Food, *Developing Human Resourcefulness,* California: International Commission on Peace and Food, 1989.
4. National Knowledge Commission: Report to the Nation 2006; UGC, A Brief Report of the National Conference on Development of Higher Education, October, 10-11, 2007; and Report of the Commission to Advise on Renovation and Rejuvenation of Higher Education, 2009.
5. Thomas Joseph, "Commission Versus Commission in Higher Education", *Economic and Political Weekly,* December 15, 2007, p. 20.
6. R. Ramachandran, "University Business", *Frontline*, July 17, 2009, p. 4.
7. T.K. Rajalakshmi, "The Increase Explained: Interview with S.K. Thorat UGC Chairperson", *Frontline,* July 17, 2009, pp. 14-15.
8. Ravi Sharma, "Main Markets", *Frontline,* July 17, 2009, p. 25.
9. S. Viswanathan, "Tamil Nadu", *Frontline,* July 17, 2009, p. 27.
10. R. Ramachandran, "It has to be a Constitutional Body: Interview with Yash Pal", *Frontline,* July 17, 2009, pp. 22-23.
11. M. Anandakrishnan, "Critique of Knowledge Commission", *Economic Political Weekly,* February 17, 2007, p. 558.
12. Pawan Agarwal, "From Kothari Commission to Pitroda Commission", *Economic and Political Weekly,* February 17, 2007, p. 555.
13. Edward, J. Balleisen and David, A. Moss (eds.), *Government and Markets: Towards a New Theory of Regulation,* Cambridge: Cambridge University Press, 2010.

2

Higher Education in Lower Order

Introduction

India is known for commissions and committees, commissions and omissions and commissions and kickbacks. Education is not exempted from this malaise of corruption. It is deeply entrenched in corrupt practices which draws the attention of every stakeholder in this domain. Recently appointed committees on Higher Education have exposed the drawbacks and weakness in the Indian Higher Education System[1] and indicated the remedial measures which are contested by several stakeholders from their own perspectives. Even among the reports of the committees one will find contradictions[2]. The prime contradiction emanates from the basic argument whether education is to produce better citizens to humanize the society or to produce marketable manpower to make products for the market. Higher Education institutions or more precisely the universities are not only to produce technocrats, medical practitioners and managers. If one looks back and evaluates the observations of the commissions and committees of the past constituted to review higher education, it is clear that education has to serve the human society in all its needs and to make our society a socialistic one. Our founding fathers had kept in mind that education had to be designed in such a way that it would help to reconstruct the society as ours is unequal and diverse in every aspect. Our higher education system had been conceptualized and shaped to reconstruct the Indian society. But now from the recommendations of the present committees and commissions, the most important of which is the Knowledge Commission, one perceives that production of manpower needed for the market is the main mandate of education at this point of time. The whole exercise has to be done is to achieve knowledge economy and that will be done in an inclusive way. The very statement of creating knowledge economy and inclusion is contradictory: the knowledge economy will create an unbridgeable gap and how will it include the excluded? No doubt higher education in India is deeply afflicted by a malaise[3]. Of all the weaknesses, making it a tradable and marketable commodity and thereby allowing the private players without having any control or supervision to make profit and exploit the people is the greatest tragedy we witness in the higher education system in India. Even during the British days education was in service and now perfectly it is in business in vulgar form and it is allowed to determine the quality of education in India. What happened to the argument of Adam Smith on the invisible hand to regulate the market? We have seen the market ethics in the recent past: how unethically players operated the economy in the world and thereby created havoc in the economy of the countries. In India education is put in the market.

Education was conceptualized very well in ancient India on par with the West. It was during the colonial administration that systemic production of manpower for government service through higher education system was started. And even after India attained independence and over a period of time the western education system permeated into our society, pushing the Indian system of education to the background. The British had not only subjugated the people of India through their administration but also the knowledge base of the people through their educational system. Whether it is West or East, at present in the context of Globalization education has to produce needed manpower with values and responsibility to achieve development in the society and thereby enable the human society to lead a decent, dignified, happy human life without subjugating degrading and denigrating each other either individually or collectively. But globalization has created unfathomable opportunity to make use of technology to produce marketable goods and services to the whole of the world with cheap labour available in the south. To cater to the needs huge manpower with precision and quality is needed. Thus to handle technology and market we require manpower. In the same way to handle socio-economic problems emerging out of the new context we need equal amount of manpower. Thus we target the educational institution to produce the needed manpower with multiple players by following the Western argument that private players will perform the task better than the public institutions with values and social responsibilities as they witness in their countries to reach the target. While looking at the argument of the West on any issue one will find harmonious integration of the new proposition and the interest of the West.

Expansion of the system and the institutions over a period since Independence are not sudden and they are systematic, gradual and scientific to some extent. Our objective now is to capture the market for which we have opened up the gates without much planning. Thus we have witnessed mushroom growth of educational institutions. Ultimately as a result we are in a position to state that we have increased the allocation of public resources for higher education and multiplied the institutions with the participation of private players to deliver goods, and to increase the output and yet we could not make a statement that we have produced the needed quality manpower suitable to the industry and the market. No one can dispute the efforts of the state in terms of the increased allocation of resources, effective policy prescription evolved and building of institutions. But the problem lies elsewhere. Rule application is more important than rule making. Thus absolutely educational administration is in a mess. While looking at the implication of the efforts taken by the Government of India in the recent past in the education sector, one will find the poor achievement from the perspective of expectation. Quality manpower production is our target and goal. On that count we have failed miserably. But our overall educational achievements in the given context more specifically in quantity are laudable[4].

In the whole process of sudden expansion an exploitative private players without any background to serve in education and commitment suddenly and schematically entered into the domain and hugely exploited the society by dubious means by using all weaknesses in the regulatory bodies which regulate the higher education system[5]. The new found aspiration to achieve prosperity and development among the middle class and new middle class has been totally exploited by the new players in higher education. As a result new educational industry has emerged in the society with the basic objective of making profit and the stakeholders turned to be an effective and aggressive consumers rather than development participants with values and social responsibilities. Is it the way to further our educational system? What ails our higher education system? And how are we going to remedy the system? It is necessary that one has to analyze the whole system in an integrated perspective. But in reality, in India we look at issues very narrowly and in isolation without having perspectives and long term goals to achieve development.

Context and Background

Our higher education system was established on the solid recommendations of the committees and commissions created for the establishment of university system in India. With lofty ideals the higher educational institutions were created. In the year 1947, Jawaharlal Nehru while delivering the special convocation address in Allahabad made the following observation:

> "A University stands for humanism, for tolerance, for reason, for progress, for the adventure of ideas and for the search for truth. It stands for the onward march of the human race towards even higher objectives. If the universities discharge their duty adequately, then it is well with the nation and the people. But if the temple of learning itself becomes a home of narrow bigotry and petty objectives, how then will the nation prosper or people grow in stature?"

The above statement is the base and basic framework of our higher learning institutions. Subsequently a whole lot of regulatory and advisory authorities were created in India both at feudal and regional levels. Policy documents were prepared to guide the higher learning institutions. Though steadily the higher education institutions have been expanded, contrary to expectation they have started declining in terms of the quality of their outputs within twenty years of their existence since their inception.

No doubt our higher education system had been slowly deteriorating over a period of time. At this point of time our governance leaders fixed the target of expansion at quantum jump. The propelling engine of expansion of higher education at present is globalization. This expansion should not be seen in isolation. It is the target of expansion for the whole world requirement. It is not an Indian phenomenon but a world phenomenon. For the expansion of the market activities, world requires huge manpower.

Manpower for Knowledge Economy

A new economy has emerged out of knowledge which is called "knowledge economy". Preparing the needed manpower at the quickest possible time-frame is the mandate of the higher education system. The needed manpower is the quality manpower. For market economy manpower need is in technology and management domain. Equally the booming economy provided opportunity for the people who have developed capability and capacity to earn unfathomable measure of profit which ultimately increases the value of life. Thus health sector also emerges as a major giant and thus technology, medicine and management have emerged as prime sectors. As a result one will find knowledge economy and a new economy of scale have emerged. Having seen the emerging potentials, the Government of India and the State Governments have started allowing the private players to move into the domain of education as the governments did not have adequate resources to invest in education to expand it to the level of requirement.

New Rich in Neo-Liberal Policy

Private players have also noticed the potentials and opportunities in the education sector. Some of the business houses and individuals saw the great opportunity to make huge profit more than what they earn from the industries and business. Further they have noticed the total weakness in the administrative set up of the education department of the governments. By making use of the weaknesses the new rich has exploited the higher education system to make steep profit. Because the regulatory agencies themselves are involved in corrupt practices. When the entire decision making arena is chocked in corruption one cannot expect the education system be freed from corruption. Here one has to remember that all private agencies here not involved in surplus money making business. There are private agencies, who maintain high standard, who have been in the field for several decades. These agencies are performing their roles very well despite volley of problems they face in the context of commercialization of education. In this context one has to clearly understand the service and disservice done by the private sector in higher education in the recent past.

No doubt by participating in higher education, they produced technical manpower for the market[6]. At the same time, the private sector has found it an instrument to make profit as they do it in industry. The proportion of profit is also very high more than what they have earned in industry.[7] In real term they consider that it is also an industry. Hence by violating all established ethical norms the private players have started exploiting the aspirants. All the regulatory bodies have also been lured into the process of expansion and as a result all regulatory bodies have lost their moral authority. Once the regulatory bodies acted as leaders of higher education gave direction and shown the way to the educational institutions have turned to be dealers of higher education.

Production of Unemployables

There is yet another issue one has to see in higher education system now: the entry of weak players with an objective of exploiting the opportunity within the shortest period have started institutions and produced manpower without even the minimum requisite quality. These students are really a liability and add to the unemployable category. Yet another point is also to be noted here that even after this much of expansion the needed manpower is not created as per demand of the market. Hence there is a mismatch between the need and the supply. This issue has to be addressed effectively to make use of the opportunity created in twenty first century[8]. The higher educational institutions have not produced quality manpower needed to industry and service sectors but it produced sizeable poor quality manpower. By producing poor quality manpower, the unemployed army has been increased and thereby it increased the problems of the society. Any sudden change or transformation will bring both positives and negatives. To keep the changes positive by mitigating the negative effects, serious steps are needed. Globalization has created opportunities and threats and both are in an unprecedented way. To make use of the opportunities and to avoid threats series of steps are needed.

Here it is to be noted that the whole of expansion is visualized only in the professional domains and more of technology, medicine and management. Market expansion activities will certainly create impact both in government and society. To work in the domain of governance and society we need more professionals and obviously we do not find such a kind of preparation. Whatever benefits we get out of technology, medicine and management, ultimately they are for society. Hence social engineering is a part and it is an integral part of the transformation. It is a moot question whether manpower is created for social engineering along with technology and medicine. One could visualize problems and crises due to development. How to tackle development crises? No doubt education is an instrument to trigger development and at the same time it has to help humanity to go for higher level activities in the process of social evolution. Whether the education we pursue has enabled the society to achieve prosperity and peace to all segments of the society. The present crisis in development, democracy, governance, and administration needs solution and it requires capacitated and skilled manpower. Against the backdrop higher education is being booked at.

Status and Reality

For meaningful intervention and correction, a realistic, perspective and an objective evaluation of our higher education system is needed. In this section we have to do this exercise. In the last sixty years, quantitative growth of higher level institutions is highly impressive. Universities have been increased from 25 to 519, colleges have been increased from 700 to 26000, teachers have been increased from 15000 to 5.05 lakh and students strength has been increased from one lakh to 11.5 lakh. The quantitative expansion is highly impressive and spectacular. One cannot be complacent with the quantity production of manpower. Our production of manpower could be seen through the process of absorption and rejection in the job market. Contrary to expectation we have not produced quantum quality manpower. As a result unemployed army has increased its size. In strict terms they are not unemployed but they are unemployable as market demands manpower continuously.

The problem in higher education draws the attention only now even though deterioration had started in higher education long back. But the problem arose intensively only during the last three years as the expansion is spectacular. It was 440 universities and 20,677 colleges in 2008 and the number has gone up to 519 and 25,951 respectively in 2010. The whole increase of the institutions is due to the target of Gross Enrolment Ratio (GER) of 15 per cent by 2012 by the Government of India. The Government of India has fixed the target of GER by various means. One cannot deny the efforts taken by the government to address these issues in higher education due to the gaps in enrolment between rural and urban, male female, low and high income groups. In the same way government tried to address the issues of poor quality and quantity of infrastructure, and poor quality of teachers. Allocation of resources to Higher Education System has been increased ten-fold from Rs. 9,500 crores in tenth Five Year Plan to Rs. 85,000 crores in eleventh Five Year Plan. The basic goal of the higher education system is to enhance the GER from the current level of 11 per cent to 21 per cent at the end of the Eleventh Five Year Plan.

Despite all the efforts, the higher education system is afflicted with deep malaise as the institutions and the stakeholders have not taken the higher education to the desired direction. Mere enhancement of allocation of resources, cosmetic changes through the existing dilapidated institutional structures, creation of certain national institutions in the existing structural condition and inviting the foreign institutions to start their campuses in India will not correct the educational system. It needs a fundamental change which is topsy-turvy in nature[9]. It has to start from law through policies and programmes. Further it should pass through institutional culture. Above all, they are all to be well regulated, managed and evaluated thoroughly for system correction then and there. In such a way the higher education system has to be placed.

Here it is to be noted that opportunities are sky high for the society to bring socio-economic development through higher education system at present because of the new dispensation 'Globalization'. To make use of the opportunity we have to gear up the system and its stakeholders to the new heights which are far from the existing reality. The Knowledge Commission Report (2006) makes it clear that "the challenges that confront higher education in India are clear. It needs a massive expansion of opportunities for higher education, to 1500 universities nationwide, that would enable India to attain a gross enrolment ratio of 15 per cent by 2015. It is just as important to raise the average quality of higher education in every sphere. At the same time, it is essential to create institutions that are exemplars of excellence at par with the best in the world. In the pursuit of these objectives, providing people with access to higher education in a socially inclusive manner is imperative. The realization of these objectives, combined with access would not only develop the skills and capabilities we need for the economy but would also help transform India into a knowledge economy and society." Over a period of time our higher education system instead of improving its quality has started deteriorating at the cost of Indian society. It had been indicated by Kothari Commission in 1964 itself. It remarked that "the situation in higher education was unsatisfactory and even alarming in some ways, that even the average standards have been falling and rapid expansion has resulted in lowering quality". An important observation has to be made here. Even though the fall of higher education in quality and substance had been indicated from the later sixties, no consistent effort on the part of the policy making and regulatory bodies to set right and they continued to facilitate quantitative expansion further now expansion has been accelerated in geometric proportion. Now we talk about surgery for the whole system. Our higher education system is far away from the industry, market, society and core values of Indian society. It distanced itself from the realities of the domains where they are preparing the manpower. Absolutely our higher education system has emerged as yet another exploitative system in India without much contribution to the society and economy. It is not facing the challenges from the stakeholders.

Vibrant Linkages

At the same time one would find the contributions of the premier institutions in terms of manpower in a smaller measure. But when market expansion demands huge manpower, we have expanded the higher education system with the involvement of the private sector. China is the best example to quote here. To make use of the new opportunity, China has expanded its higher education system but the expansion is steady compared to India. It is being well regulated. Moreover the Chinese higher education system's connection with industry and society is very intensive, meaningful and contributory for both. It works in industrial reality and social reality. In overall evaluation and assessment, our higher education system also has expanded institutionally and structurally and thereby produced quantum jump of manpower. But in terms of quality, it does not reflect the needed improvement and instead it declined drastically. While making disaggregate analysis one will find the premier institutions are in tune with the expectation of production of quality manpower to the market. In research, even they could not deliver the output to the level of their capacity and capability and to the level of expectations.

Our university system is far away from the market and the society. Many of the Universities and their Departments are running programmes and conducting examinations and they are not doing worthwhile research and bringing quality publications. While assessing the capability of the manpower produced by the traditional higher education system through research it is to be noted that a sizeable number of students passing out from the universities are not to the level of the expectation of the market. Further it is to be noted that substantial Research and Development did not take place in the higher educational institutions for the Industries, Markets and Society. It is a major gap which is pushing the higher educational system far away from the reality and facing the challenges. The challenges of the industries, markets and the society are being faced and tackled only by the industrial houses, market institutions and governing institutions respectively and not jointly with higher educational institutions. This gap made the industrial houses to create more research units in their own industries and training institutions to train manpower within their industrial houses.

If higher education system is strong, vibrant, capable to face the challenges in the industries the needed Research and Development for industries will be conducted and carried out in the higher educational institutions with the financial support of the industries and thereby there will be a strong linkage between the university and industries. It takes place very rarely. In the same way the social and economic problems never get discussed for policy making in the arena of higher educational institutions. After the onset of globalization, social and economic problems are intense and prone to more conflicts which require new policies, solutions and programmes. But they are not being either discussed or debated in the higher educational institutions for either knowledge's sake or for policy advocacy. Even though the universities have organised workshops, conferences and seminars, the substantial recommendations and observations are taken into account seriously by the policy making bodies they do not reflect the reality. Yet they serve the purpose of career promotion for the teachers. Since the academic institutions are far away from the social reality, the bureaucrats and policy makers never connect themselves with universities for advocacy. From the perspective of the policy makers and bureaucrats, academics are not useful for policy advocacy.

Of course, a few academics are useful since they are most inevitable persons and hence they are being made members in the government committees and commissions. Thus higher educational institutions are not linked with social realities, industrial realities and context realities[10]. It is a considered opinion that our educational institutions in the name of autonomy are far away from the realities and they do not have requisite commitments and capability to work on the problems of the society. The teachers working in the higher learning institutions have reduced their space of operation and narrowed themselves to classrooms. As a result one can easily notice the gap between the book view and the field view. Dr. S. Radhakrishnan made a significant remark about our higher education system in the formative years of independence. It is worth remembering here. He stated that "there is a need for change in the perception and attitude of universities realizing that their field is wider, task is greater and goal is higher in building a strong and happy India. The universities are not merely places of conferring degrees and distinctions. They besides being places of learning, are also centres of service and wholesome development of human personality; of men and women, turning them into fine human beings. The universities cannot stand isolated; they should be active participants in development activities, which are benevolent and beneficial for people. It is unfortunate that the hopes, aspirations and expectations of students are not fulfilled to the extent expected. Therefore, it is time to mend and amend the systems which have a negative effect on the society". He made a penetrating analysis of our university system. One could see the relevance of his observation even today. A society has to be constructed, reconstructed, modernized and made to live peacefully and prosperously with proper guidance and governance and for which intellectual and knowledge input is the basis and this knowledge input will be generated only from higher educational institutions. The moot question is whether our educational institutions are really in that mould to shape our society and governance.

In a place where a medical college is functioning, high incidence of MMR, IMR, malnutrition of children, high percentage of women and adolescent girls are affected by anaemia, insanitation are being witnessed. What is the impact it has created in the society where the institution is functioning. In a place where an engineering college is functioning, high incidence of irregular water supply, wastage of water, frequent disrepair of motors pumping water, faulty laying of pipelines, poor quality of drainage construction, failure of biogas plant, poor quality of roads, and so on. It means the Engineering

College has no connection with the society where it is functioning. In the same way other colleges. Absolutely the higher educational institutions do not have either forward linkage with the policy making and decision making or backward linkages with society where they function.

A system can produce quality manpower only when they work in reality. Society, polity, economy are dynamic. They are to be observed and absorbed in our activities. The changes we found in social realities have to be incorporated in our academic activities. To work in reality, the higher educational system has to work in three different domains, namely academic (teaching), research and outreach (extension) integrally and organically. It has to work in knowledge domain and then only it can contribute to the policy making. It has to link with the reality and then only it can work on the need. Higher education system has to emerge as vibrant unit from deep slumber. It should make itself an inevitable player in policy making and decision making.

Our universities are teaching and examination conducting centres and not as centre of research and learning. That is the reason why our quality publication has gone down drastically whereas the quality publication has gone up in China. Even in Ph.D. production, we have improved in absolute numbers but not in percentage and compared to China we are low in production of Ph.D. thesis. Further the quality of research has gone down. The university system requires strong leadership. The Leadership is from the top-Minister for Human Resource Management to the bottom—the head of a Department in an University or College. Be it a Minister or a Secretary or a Vice-Chancellor or a Principal or a Head of the Department, everyone has to contribute substantially for the effective functioning of higher learning institutions. But unfortunately now they are under the political influence. People with poor academic credentials have entered into the university as Vice-Chancellors without having any commitment, perspective and understanding. They are unable to provide leadership. But they act as not leaders but as dealers of education business. Since they are the political appointees, mediocre teachers entered into the teaching of the university through political pressure. Now it has gone to the level of appointing Vice-Chancellors on the basis of bribe given by the candidates. It is being debated openly. It is not being contested either by the Governments or by the Chancellors who are appointing the Vice-Chancellors. As a result naturally the Vice-Chancellors have to manage to get the invested sum within the stipulated period of three or five years. In the university system there are two ways to manage money easily. One is through construction activities and other one is recruitment of staff. One can easily visualize what will be the quality of construction and the teachers. Teachers are in the executive authority of the Universities. They can play their constructive role in effectively preventing the erosion of values and responsibilities of the Universities. The teachers who are in the executive boards never perform their objective roles. Instead they always perform the role which will serve the best interests of the teaching community as they are mostly elected by them. Thus teachers also join with the groups which exploit the society by not performing their effective role legitimately in the decision making bodies of the Universities.

In order to maintain quality in higher education system, NAAC was created. It has covered not even one-third of the universities and colleges in terms of their evaluation. As per the evaluation of the NAAC, best performed institutions are the Deemed Universities but as per the evaluation committee of the Human Resource Development Ministry, the Deemed Universities are the poor institutions to deliver educational service in this country. God only knows the truth. Both evaluations are done by the academics. Further a country has to be guided properly through the policy guidelines. The policy guidelines are being prepared and they are to be followed by all the institutions from regulatory institutions to higher learning institutions. But now even the policy formulating institutions are in contradiction and conflict. They are being discussed openly. The contradiction between the HRD and UGC is obvious through the reports produced by these two. The regulatory authorities of the higher education system have lost their moral stature as they exhibited corrupt practices in their dealings and it has gone to the level of arresting the leaders of these institutions. How the system is going to be corrected? At any cost it is to be corrected[11].

Integrated Analysis

No one has denied that Indian Higher Education has expanded and produced quantum manpower. The question is not on the quantity but on the quality. The quality of the manpower is not to the level of the expectation of the market. No one has denied the private sector's contribution is hither education. The question is on the profit making approach of the new rich used the neo-liberal policy in higher education sector. No one denies the role of the state in expansion of higher education through its policies and resource allocation. The question is on politicization of the higher education through political influence and appointing mediocre people as Vice-Chancellors as managers instead of leaders of the institutions. No one denies the higher learning institutions capacity and capability in terms of its structure and staff, but the question is on their output and outcome in the society as there is no role for these institutions to face the challenges of the society. Our university system in the name of specialization, integrality of knowledge is lost as we have University for Technology, University for Medicine, University for Agriculture, University for Science and so on which exclude the multiplicity of disciplines and as a result human values are lost as Humanity and Social Sciences are excluded in the learning process. All sciences and technologies are Human Sciences and technologies are for human well-being. It is not integrated in our university system and it is the tragedy in our higher education system. Yet another tragedy is that the higher education system has not created space for growth and development of Indigenous Knowledge Skill and Science. A society could not have existed in history without a skill and knowledge base. India had that knowledge base equivalent to that of the West. Nalanda and Taxila were the great examples. In our higher education system we have not created scope for it. The Rural University System created in the country was for development of skill, knowledge, science, technology based on the indigenous practices. At the same time Rural University System integrates the best elements of the Western higher education system which is vogue in India.

The outdated university structure and practices have to be revamped through laws both at the Centre and the States. The Higher Education system should be made integral part of the development process of the society for which the academic, research and extension programmes have to be chalked out through a process of conscious and continuous interaction between the higher education system and industry, market, and society. This interactive process will enable the higher education system to face the challenges in the respective domains.

The present role of the teachers is being criticized as they keep themselves away from the social realities. For revolution or transformation or rejuvenation and for every change the role of teachers are imperative. Today their role in all those processes is minimum. Unless the teachers take up the active role through academic, research and outreach programmes, the high learning institutions cannot be made vibrant and relevant to the transformative and development process. Thus the whole system needs a thorough overhauling.

First and foremost the subject "education" has either to be in central list or it should be in state list. Preferably it should be in the state list as originally it was in state subject. Otherwise state will happily put the blame on the centre on each and every ill witnessed in the higher education sector. Further the states will also contribute for deterioration without taking any responsibility. It is the high time to make the state governments responsible for education. Secondly, a clear cut higher education policy has to be evolved. It should be with the cooperation and approval of the state governments. The regulatory bodies have to be strengthened by appointing giants in the respective bodies and by which the image of the institutions can be enhanced. Creating more number of higher education institutions such as colleges and universities are so important and equally strengthening the existing institutions by financing the higher education for improving the infrastructure facilities. A compulsory linkage between higher education institutions and industry higher education institutions and market and higher education institutions and society have to be created. It should be made mandatory in the policy document itself. Any evaluation of higher learning institutions should be based on the indicators in all these three domains. Universities have to concentrate on research, advocacy and outreach programmes. Higher education institutions have to perform the tasks of teaching, research and outreach programmes in an integrated way. Quality of teaching has to be improved. The existing teaching mode has to be changed to learning mode. Further use of technology for teaching has to be made mandatory. Outdated programmes have to be weeded out. Need based programmes have to be designed innovatively and they are to be imparted very effectively. While designing the programmes, the involvement of the stakeholders outside the university system who can substantially contribute for designing the programme could be integrated into the Board of Studies of the University System. Higher education institutions have to transform the teaching nuances from the existing practices which are outmoded and unattractive to the students. Universities have to be liberated from the bureaucratic clutches. Sizeable reduction of non-teaching staff will enable the University system to emerge successfully. It could be done only through governance reform at the University level. Governance arrangements have to be transformed to suit the requirements. Accountability mechanism has to be strengthened. Governance reform could be made effectively only by appointing very effective leaders as Vice-Chancellors. More managers and dealers cannot perform the new task of transformation. Now in many of the universities, we find only brokers and dealers and not leaders. It is the most crucial point for transforming higher learning institutions. One among the senior professors can be appointed Vice-Chancellor for a period of three years as we have the practice of appointing Heads of Departments and Deans of Schools. By doing so the leadership will be effective as it is a collective leadership. Cost of education has to be made affordable even to the poor.

Conclusion

The subject education should be either in central list or state list. It should not be in concurrent list as we find it today. Preferably it should be in the state list. Because both the Centre and the State are blaming each other for the deteriorating conditions of the higher education in India. Higher education system should be effectively monitored and supervised by which accountability has to be ensured. A new education policy has to be evolved to overcome the confusion in higher education system to give direction to the system. The educational institutions have to be made to face the challenges of the industry, market and society and they should be made to respond to the challenges. An effective linkage has to be established between the higher learning institutions and society, industry and market effectively and synergistically. The synergetic linkage aspect has to be made mandatory for higher learning institutions. The regulatory authorities have to be revamped and by which moral stature of the authority has to be restored and enhanced. Vice-Chancellors have to be appointed from among the faculty members of the same university as Chief Secretary is appointed for the State Government. Universities should be given mandatory stipulation that the academic, research and outreach programmes have to be conducted in an integrated way rather in isolation. The universities have to be relieved from conducting academic programmes and examinations. Universities have to conduct intensive research and outreach programmes. Hence a new policy has to be evolved and proper preparation has to be done in the university system both structurally and functionally. Teachers have to be prepared for a new culture of change. Aspirants (Students) attitude has to be changed towards the goal of higher education.

Notes and References

1. National Knowledge Commission, *National Knowledge Commission: Report of The Nation 2006*, New Delhi: Govt. of India, 2006; University Grants Commission, *A Brief Report of The National Conference on Development of Higher Education,* New Delhi: University Grants Commission, 2007; MHRD, *Report of The Commission to Advise on Renovation and Rejuvenation of Higher Education,* New Delhi Government of India, 2009.
2. Thomas Joseph, "Commission versus Commission in Higher Education" *Economic and Political Weekly,* December 15, 2007.
3. Pawan Agarwal, "From Kothari Commission to Pitroda Commission" *Economic and Political Weekly,* February 17, 2007.
4. Beena Shah, "Indian Higher Education: New Horizons and Plausible Challenges ...Wilting a Way AHEAD", *University News,* Vol. 48: No. 28, July 12-18, 2010, p. 64.
5. G. Planithurai, "Higher Education in India: Where are we leading", *University News,* Vol. 48:, No. 28, July 12-18, 2010, pp. 22-23.
6. M. Ananda Krishnan, "Critique of Knowledge Commission", *Economic and Political Weekly* (February 17, 2007), p. 558.
7. R. Ramachandran, "University Business", *Frontline,* July 17, 2009, p. 4.
8. UNESCO "Learning: The Treasure Within" *Report to UNESCO of The International Commission on Education for Twenty First Century,* Paris: UNESCO, 1996.
9. Ministry of Human Resource Development, *Report of the Committee to Advise on Renovation and Rejuvenation of Higher Education,* New Delhi: Govt. of India, 2009.
10. G. Planithurai, "Rural Universities in the Era of Globalization"; *University News,* Vol. 47: No. 33 (August, 2009); G. Planithurai, "Larger Role of Academics in Rural Human Life", *University News* Vol. 47: No. 16, (April, 2009).
11. Kapil Sibal, Minister for Human Resource Development made a Commitment that Structural Reform will be within 100 days. Till date we could not see any improvement, *Front line* (July 17, 2009).

3

System and Stakeholders in Higher Education in India

The Context

Today's Higher Education System is afflicted by an array of diseases and disabilities and, as a result, what has to be delivered by the system has not been delivered. Once the task of the Higher Education System was to prepare citizens for a just society but now it is to prepare marketable human resource. Preparing marketable human resource is unequivocally the prime objective of higher education system. Once even during the days of British Administration in India it was treated as a service and now it turned to be an industry. It is highly competitive industry and it has started violating all ethical norms. All regulatory bodies have failed miserably to regulate the higher educational institutions as they are deeply crept into the corrupt practices. All the regulatory bodies have also lost their moral stature and credibility. As a result the total higher education system is in deep crisis. One has to analyze the reasons for such a crisis. Globalisation has opened huge opportunities for human resource and it resulted in sudden expansion of higher education system. Generally people attribute that in any sudden expansion of institutions or organizations normally such type of deviations and dilution of standard bound to happen. Realistically reasons are being examined through management system, policy options, legal and legislative options and administrative perspectives. Higher education system is with different agencies. It is with public, private and public private partnership. Some will perceive that problems arose because of the entry of the private. Private agencies entered into the system because of the failure of the public institutions. Beyond certain limit public could not expand. Even in the existing public institutions are facing plethora of problems. Along with the existing disabilities the higher education system received another jolt by the entry of the privates and now foreign institutions are coming through the new policy options like globalization, liberalization and privatization adopted by the Governments both Centre and the States.

Any new adventure or scientific and technological inventions will have both positive and negative effects on the society. The implications are the results of the handling of the same by the humanity. No doubt the Globalisation process triggered both opportunities and threats. An intelligent and sensitive society will make use of the opportunities and avoid threats of Globalisation. Unfortunately the existing regulatory mechanism could not withstand the pressure of Globalisation and it broke out and as a result the whole system is in anarchy, chaos and corruption. But it function as a system. Yet it produced unprecedented changes in the market, governance and society. It has got both positive and negative impacts. Who gains and who lost is the basic question. Even in the chaotic and anarchical conditions one would find a lot of benefits to the people and economy. It cannot be undermined and underestimated. For the global need of manpower, the new partners in higher education have produced the volume of manpower however weak in terms of quality the manpower produced by the new partners is. This achievement cannot be possible without the new partners. The new partners have certainly contributed substantially though they added problems also. The problems could have been tackled very effectively for the advantage of all provided the regulatory mechanisms repositioned well to the context and the new requirements. But the new partners have helped only to the rich or those who took risks in borrowing money and made use of this new opportunity. By taking into account the positive effects, the government and the stakeholders try to find solutions to minimize the negatives and maximize the positives.

The issues have to be tackled through new policy initiatives, new regulatory mechanisms, managerial solutions, administrative reforms and legal remedies in the higher education system. The above remedial actions have to be taken synergistically both by the Centre and the State Governments as education is in the concurrent list.

Globalisation has not only affected the higher education system but also the entire education system from pre-primary to higher education system. Because peoples aspiration to prosperity has increased and they wanted to make use of the new opportunities. If it is to be done without corrupt practices and exploitation the education system has to be corrected and streamlined. In the same way the authorities created through law and decisions of the governments have to regulate and to manage the institutions effectively and efficiently to cater to the needs of all segments of the society. Broadly speaking the damages done to higher education institutions have to be tackled only by the higher level authorities. All the regulatory bodies have to be reorganized and regain their moral authority. Positions of these bodies have been at present politicized and the corrupt practices in those offices have brought down the name and hence the moral stature has to be regained. Now instead of acting firmly governments are blaming each other for not regulating the system. One can find lapses in handling of these institutions by both Centre and State Governments. By seeing the weak position of the governments, the new players in higher education, namely the private sector took advantage and exploited the market.

All the above problems are in the domain of higher education and slowly they have crept into the entire education system. How to tackle all the above problems? All the above problems are to be tackled only by the governments. They are not in my hands. I always look at problems from a different perspective. For any problem I look at it from my perspective. Can we correct ourselves first if we are in the process as stakeholders. Being a teacher in the university system what I have to do to correct the maladies is to be pondered over. What could be done at my level as I have a space to act? Further am I discharging the duties and responsibilities as expected by the system and the stakeholders? What can I be in this context as a responsible teacher instead of blaming the system and the environment without contributing anything substantially to correct the present maladies. Of course, they are to be changed and for which teachers have to work. But as teachers we have to ask ourselves whether we have performed our roles properly and discharged all our responsibilities. For many of the ills in the system we are also responsible and we have paved way for such a kind of anarchical situation in higher education system. Before cleansing our system first we have to correct ourselves and we must begin reform from ourselves. I use to think to what extent I can discharge my duties perfectly and to what extent I can work for changing the environment and reforming the institutions collectively. I may meet with failures in changing the environment and reforming the institutions while doing it collectively. But I may not fail in perfecting myself and in discharging my duties and responsibilities in context to the expectations.

Corrective steps are needed and they are the imperatives for streamlining and overhauling the entire system. May be in one respect the above argument may seem to be acceptable but in reality it cannot be accepted in totality as systems are functioning with system facilitators and system managers and it involves a sizeable segment of the communities as stakeholders. Without their active support system cannot function. I am of the opinion based on experience that systems malfunctioning is always with the collusion of the stakeholders and with the passive inaction of the stakeholders. It is applicable not only to the higher educational system and it is applicable to all systems and sub-systems. Over a period of time insensitiveness has been developed among the people to be passive for any malfunctioning. Non-adherence to laws is being discussed but the real problem lies not in enactment of laws or implementation of laws but in that absence of a law abiding culture. So to correct any system, the role of the stakeholders is important. Here in higher education system I am referring to the teachers and the beneficiaries as stakeholders. They have to play a vital role in the process of system correction. Of course, barring a few they are not active participants in the process rather they remain as spectators to look at the functioning passively. The stakeholders have also added fuel to the existing fire in the higher educational system by not performing their role as teacher in terms of professional teaching, socially relevant research and conducting impact making outreach programmes apart from non-performing the function of correction of the system. Specifically the three roles to be performed by the teachers are being explained in this paper. After discussing the performance of the teachers in the above roles, I will suggest some ways and means to improve the existing conditions.

Roles to be Performed

A teacher has three roles to perform in any institution where she/he is employed. They are teaching, research and outreach activities. In higher educational institutions, they have to teach students, carryout research activities and outreach programmes. If a teacher wants to become a scholar, it is necessary for him/her to pursue teaching, research and outreach programmes integrally, consciously and continuously and professionally. Then only the teaching life will be enriching, meaningful, rewarding and enjoyable. A teacher has to connect himself or herself with students and more deeply into the subject to know the truth and to connect himself or herself with society meaningfully. Teachers whether they are Assistant Professors or Associate Professors or Professors all their activities are to be carried out very professionally and sharply as professionals and they have to perform the tasks whether it is teaching or research or outreach professionally to get the results as we target. To become a professional one has to be more focused on the skills and knowledge on a particular area as expected to fulfil the tasks. Simply speaking result oriented activities have to be done. The teachers have to equip themselves to cater to the needs of the expectations of the stakeholders. What are the expectations of the stakeholders? The students who are getting into the portals of higher education are having a perspective that they should become employable. Acquiring knowledge is also essential but now it is not the main target. To become employable the prorgramme has to help the students. When educational programmes are designed, objectives and goals of programmes and courses are to be fixed. To realize the objectives and goals of the programmes, the programmes and courses have to be imparted. In order to create an impact the needed skills and capacity among the teachers are essential and imperative. The teachers have to equip themselves in terms of teaching skill. It does not mean the verbal communication skill. It requires the capacity to handle modern equipments and instruments. The teacher should have grip over the subjects they teach and the subjects are their area of specialization at a higher level. It is not mere taking notes from the books and delivering the same in the classroom. It is a tape recorder work. It should be something creative. Hence, the teacher has to evaluate and assess the level of the students in terms of their learning capacity, assimilation capacity and comprehension capacity and communication capacity. To suit the requirements of the students, teachers have to prepare themselves and impact the programme. It is not ninety working days, forty contact hours, three cumulative formative assessment tests and final three hours end semester examination conducted for the students to evaluate the students in a course or a programme. It is a process oriented exercises and not target oriented.

For a programme or a subject or a course we design some rationale or objectives or goals. After undergoing this course or programme it is perceived that the students will be equipped on certain key aspects of the subjects we taught as mentioned in the course objectives. But while imparting the course and programme the teachers are not keeping their eyes on the rationale fixed for the subject but they are more particular about the three tests, end semester examinations and classroom lectures but not the assessment of the outcome expected in the whole exercise. To illustrate this principle I can draw an example. A student undergoing a post-graduate programme has to take up a course in the second semester on "Project Management". The programme has its own objectives and in the same way the course has its own objectives. The objective of the course "Project Management" reads as "after undergoing this course the students will be able to prepare a project proposal, to implement the project at the ground, and to evaluate the project in terms of outcome and to prepare entire process report". The teacher has to impart the programme in teaching and learning mode to ensure that students constantly gaining the input needed to perform the roles as they are indicated in the objective of the course. As a result students are passing out from the institutions with certificates but not the capacity and capability as expected from the course and the programme. The whole weakness in the system is not only because of the existing syllabus packages but purely due to the poor performance of the teachers. If teachers are capable many of the ills in the system can be easily corrected. In my opinion, all the weaknesses of the educational system are being highlighted by the teachers in order to hide their weakness, poor skills and capacities. My basic argument is that there are problems which are of different kinds relating to legal, managerial, administrative, financial and so on. Of course, they are to be corrected. Yet the teachers have a major role in the system correction. If the correction starts from the teachers the system correction will be easy. How to do it? The teachers have to perform their duties as a professional. To perform very well teachers have to equip themselves as professionals. Professionalism expects skilled activity to produce results. Sharpness, focused, specialized, systematic activities are to be carried out to produce expected results. Professionalism need not necessarily be in engineering or medicine. Any subject is a professional subject if it is imparted professionally. Professionalism is not knowledge based. It is always skill based. The skill also distinguishes professionalism from non-professionalism. A non-professional course is not a non-utility course as some of the state governments declared. They are knowledge based. A society cannot progress without the base of knowledge. Knowledge and skills are imperative for development. It is unfortunate skill dominates in higher education system. Intellectual works can be done only in knowledge domain. Basically non- professional courses or programmes are the real development oriented. Skills are only for some activities. But to orient and prepare the students all programmes have to be imparted professionally. Even a non-professional course can be conducted in a professional way. Thus professionalism is a process and a way by which any activity has to be carried out. Hence all the teachers working in higher learning institutions have to orient themselves as professionals. Now-a-days we find even a professional courses are being done in a non- professional way and that is why we could not produce worthy and capable manpower to the need of the market and the society. Hence teachers are to be oriented and prepared for specialized professional task and by which the higher learning institutions can be made.

Resources Utilization

Universities have enormous facilities with huge public investment. Library, laboratories, resource centres, internet facilities, computer centres, skill clubs, language labs, special coaching centres meant for marginalized students. Many of these facilities are underutilized and sometimes they are unutilized. Huge investment has been made on all these facilities. But these facilities are being used only by a few sections of the students. The full potentials have not been utilized. These facilities are under the effective control and coordination of the teachers. But the teachers never bother about the under-utilization of these resources by the students. The teachers have to take special effort to draw the students to those facilities and make them to use all the facilities meant for them at the maximum level. One should not assume that simply by providing facilities, they will be used effectively. It is necessary to create awareness among the students about the importance of these facilities and how they are to be used. In India in all the spheres facilities and infrastructures created for public utility have not been used to the fullest potential. In the same way educational institutions have invested huge public money to create such facilities. They are to be used. Students as stakeholders should have ownership and at least they should claim over it. But it is not happening in universities. In our social and political system development has not been made as right so far. Slowly now we are moving into the domain of rights by passing historic legislations for information and education. As we had been in charity mode and approach in development, students never assert themselves to claim their entitlements as rights and students are treated as recipients of benefits. As a result, their entitlements are not claimed. In order to make the students to claim their entitlements teachers have to motivate the students and make them to effectively use the resources. Students should feel that these are their entitlements and rights and they are to be claimed as rights rather than charity and to that level awareness has to be created. Otherwise the whole investment made on these facilities are waste. This responsibility is with the teachers. To perform the above task the teachers should have more commitment and sense of responsibilities. Take for example General Library, and Department Libraries are not effectively used as the library hours are not effectively managed. In the library hours, no teacher is able to see whether the students have gone to the library or to the department library for library and reference works. Department libraries are in the hands of the teaching staff. Most of the occasions it is not functioning. Teachers normally say that it is only an additional responsibility and hence according to their convenience they run the department libraries. If a teacher is committed, he or she can get the help of a student and operate the department library very effectively. It depends on the commitment of the teachers. There are student clubs under the coordinatorship of the teachers. But these clubs are mostly non-functional. Rarely they function as on students' demand. Teachers are not taking initiative to bring students to clubs and ask them to use the clubs to improve their skills. There are coaching centres to prepare students for professional examination, JRF, and civil service examination. Even these centres are to be used professionally. Students with poor ability can also equip themselves through these centres.

We normally perceive that students need only classroom lectures and reading materials for their examinations. In reality they need much more than teaching. They need the personal attention of the teachers. For personal counselling and career guidance teachers have to help. Even in the learning process also teachers have to go with them. In our tradition we have gurukula system. It can be practiced in our educational institutions. Twenty to thirty students will be allotted to each teacher for such a kind of counselling and guidance. Many of the problems of the students can be easily solved by the guidance of the teachers. Students discipline will also be maintained well.

To perform the task the teacher has to understand the level of learning capability and according to the needs of the students course material has to be prepared and they are to be taught in appreciate mode which are suited to their needs. The whole process can be seen in the progress of learning by the students as water level of wells increases after a heavy rain. It can be seen among the students visibly and for which meaningful indicators have to be devised. To perform the above task a teacher has to be conscious of the whole process of teaching and learning. It is the product of organic process not a mechanical process. If it is done in an organic process, the fixed objectives for the programme can be reached. The whole assessment and evaluation process have to be made in such a way that the evaluation reveals the reach of the objectives by the students. Very rarely this happens as both the students and teachers are rarely in the same wavelength in understanding the programme. Many of the occasions both have involved in the process mechanically and as a result they perform the task through a set of activities but not reaching the goal. Teachers go to the class, teach the students, evaluate them in a formal way and marks are assigned and certificates are issued but the goals and objectives mentioned in the programmes are not realized. Hence we find a gap between the intent and reality. Major segment of student communities are unemployable because their skill level is very low.

That is why we say that any programme can be made professional if it is done in the way it has to be done. The teachers have to equip themselves by making use of the facilities given to them. Computers, internet connections, LCD projectors which are available for the teachers. In universities, computers are given to individual teachers. How many teachers are using the computer effectively? How many of the teachers are using the internet facilities to update themselves by connecting themselves with world through webs? And how many of the teachers are using power point presentation? If they are used effectively by the teachers, they will be equiped to cater to the needs of the students. If the teaching is done through modern devices teachers can reach out the goals sharply and professionally. It all depends on the way it is being done and not because of the nomenclature of the programme. An institute offers B.A. Social Work which receives the attention of the whole country and how it happens not because of nomenclature. It is because of the way it is being done. If a department offers a programme with the input of five teachers, it can be done professionally provided all the five teachers are professionally equipped and having professional competence and consciousness. Many of the departments got prominence only because of the professionalism they have developed. It requires good leadership for the department. In the same way if all the departments are having such professionalism, the whole institute is a professional institute. It all depends not on the policy, allocation of resources and other things and it all depends on the teachers. It requires only the needed culture, namely academic, research and outreach cultures. More particularly teachers should find their pride in his/her professionalism and specification.

Our Research Programmes

At present we face a volley of social, economic and political problems which are acute in nature and the conditions of the people more particularly poor and the marginalised are deplorable because of globalization of economy which need solution and those problems are to be addressed. The problem we face are much complicated and complex compared to the past. They are to be analysed systematically and scientifically. To analyse the problems in the society, governance, administration and development we need more of qualified researchers. All the above concepts are now contested in the new context. But we could not get qualified researchers to do social science research. The new context requires more sophisticated new methodological nuances. While going through the Ph.D. profile of the universities one will find the growing trend of research output. A university professor claims that he has produced forty Ph.D. thesis within a short span of fifteen years. But he is not able to spell out his specialization. Production of Ph.D. thesis is on the increase but they are not referred to any of the problems of society faces. Very rarely the university research is taken into consideration for decision making. Even the civil society documents are being referred to by the bureaucracy on many of the occasions. Barring a few our *universities theses are referred* to any policy advocacy in the recent past. In such a way the gap has been maintained between the research done in the universities and policy options adopted at the policy making domain to solve the socio-economic problems of our society. For the problems society faces the bureaucrats try their level best to find solution. But university teachers are in comfort zone. The officials are at risk. On the one hand we could not get qualified staff or researchers to carry out quality research but on the other we have enormous Ph.D. theses done by the research scholars in the university. Why this paradox? One thing is very clear from the existing trend. Research is seeking truth or scientifically analyzing the issues are old concepts. Now research is equated with production of Ph.Ds. Our teachers are not conscious of research responsibilities. To them it is a device by which his/her career option can be enhanced by producing more number of Ph.D. theses. A teacher can claim that she/he has produced certain number of Ph.D. theses which are mandatory for promotion. Now after the mushrooming of deemed universities, without having any infrastructure and qualified staff it admitted thousands of Ph.D. scholars. The Deemed University managements thought and found that it is an opportunity to mint money. A single university has earned six crores in enrolling Ph.D. scholars. All retired teachers are Ph.D. guides. Now university becomes Ph.D. production mill. Despite the proliferation of thesis there is no sign of using the thesis produced in the universities by policy makers. Not even 5 per cent of the theses are worth publication. Real scientific research is being done on some specialized institutes and in foreign universities on the issues of the Indian society, governance and administration. Some of the civil society organizations are far better than some of the universities in producing scientific research document. Given to the size of the academics in the academic and research institutions the available publication is very meagre. Further available quality publications is further very limited.

Outreach Programmes

In our university system we do not have an institutional structure to carryout outreach programmes popularly called extension activities. Conventionally Agriculture is the faculty meant and known for extension activities. But now even the Agriculture Departments have failed miserably in their jobs. Perspectively speaking all the departments in the system can do outreach programmes.

Outreach programmes are nothing but connecting the academic institutions with the larger society for learning purposes and to extend available extendables, namely ideas, skills, knowledge and services from the academic institutions to the society. Conventional universities treat teaching is the fundamental core responsibility but research is optional as teachers need it for their career development. To satisfy the requirement they have to supervise Ph.D. students and publish articles in research journals. But outreach programmes are not at all made mandatory and not even necessary for career development. Hence there is no primacy for extension activities. Outreach programmes are integral to teaching learning process in higher education system. The society is losing heavily from the higher education institutions and higher education institutions are losing heavily from the society. Both are losing and as a result we could not improve our quality of teaching and research as academics have no live contact with the social realities. Universities have lot of extendables in the form of ideas, skills, services, knowledge but they are not transferred to the society. Totally they are unutilized. Society provides enormous opportunities for the students and the teachers to learn from the society through live contact. In the university system in India proper institutional structures have not been established and developed to carry out meaningful outreach programmes. At the university level Department of Adult Education can perform the extension service to the communities. In reality they are not doing the role as expected and they are also not equipped skill and capacity-wise to extend the extendables from the universities to community. Absolutely universities are far away from the society. Social realities are fully understood by the students those who are interacting with the society constantly and consciously. Humanities and social science programmes have to have constant field interaction. But in today's context there is no such interaction. In Western universities, the students and teachers who are specializing in Indian studies, are coming and living with the communities for the purpose of learning. In such a way they link it with the community. In Indian universities teaching is stand alone based on secondary material. But, of course, research is for career advancement. That is why we are unable to improve our quality of teaching and research. Without exception all the departments of the universities can do extension activities in the society. By doing so the learning will be effective and more meaningful. In teaching even understanding of the subjects can be achieved by methodological nuances of teaching, but intricacies of the issues and sensitivity could be developed and achieved only by doing extension or outreach. It requires only commitment on the part of the teachers.

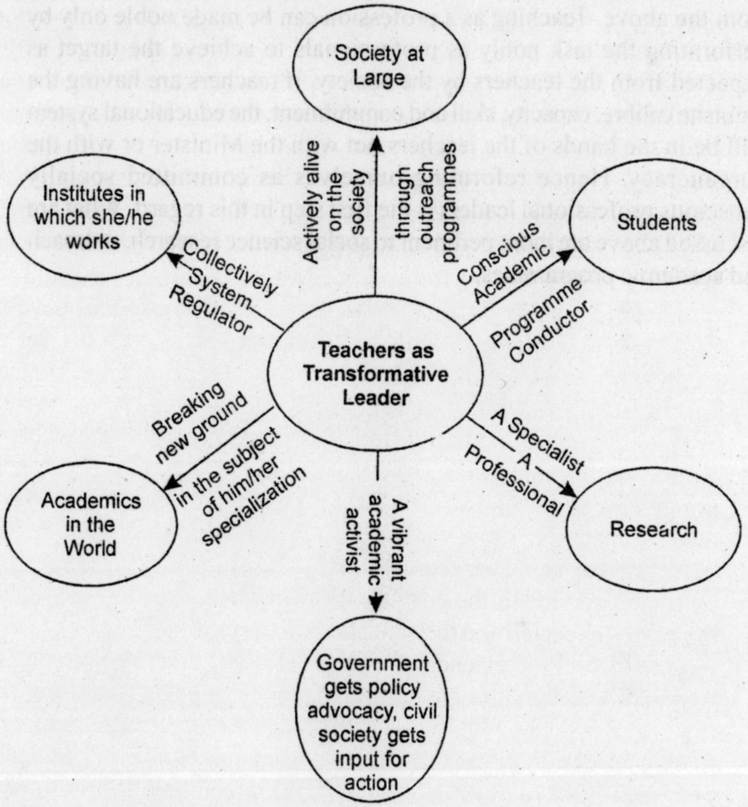

Diagram 3.1: Teachers are Transformative Leaders

Conclusion

There is no denying that some important legislations are needed, and meaningful and effective managerial system has to be in place for effective management of the higher educational institutions to set right the maladies in the higher education system. Apart from the above the teachers can reorient themselves to work for the new opportunities and to face the new challenges through teaching, research and outreach programmes. By taking initiative by teachers to perform the tasks and responsibilities assigned to them, integrally and professionally by reorienting themselves many of the ills in the system and the society can be solved. Let us start the change from us instead of expecting from the above. Teaching as a profession can be made noble only by performing the task nobly as professionals to achieve the target as expected from the teachers by the society. If teachers are having the requisite calibre, capacity, skill and commitment, the educational system will be in the hands of the teachers not with the Minister or with the bureaucracy. Hence reforming ourselves as committed socially conscious professional leaders is the first step in this regard. What are discussed above are more pertinent to social science research, outreach and academic programmes.

4

Larger Role of Academics in Rural Human Life

Introduction

At present Globalization of the economy has made life more difficult for many and enjoyable for a few segments of any society in the world. In this way life has been influenced by the activities of Globalisation around the world. The present political and economic institutions and organizations are trying to address the issues arising out of Globalization and yet they are not able to do much as the political and economic institutions have been somewhere tied up in their own framework and locked up within the liberal framework and they are unable to come out from the orbit of globalisation and look at the real issues of human misery[1]. Moreover the institutions and organizations have not equipped themselves and increased their capacity and capability to cope with the new requirements[2]. Instead, they hang around in the same place and look at the damage caused to the human society in the process of globalization and look for remedies to restore normalcy in order to restart the process of globalization with much vigour. Everyone looks at the functioning and behaviour of the institutions and identify the loopholes and they try to plug the loopholes in the process. All their discussions, deliberations and governance discourses are on the market-state relationship. But they have missed the link between the market and the people and the state and the people.

People matter much in the whole process of development[3]. The two forces, namely, the market and the state, play a very important role in managing the economy and politics. At present, the market is a powerful force. There is yet another force—state—which has to be powerful to manage the market for the advantage of the people. But, in reality, the state cannot control the market. Even in failures, the market gives directions to the state on how it should help the market to save the economy. The state has a larger role to manage the society by attending to the needs and the aspirations of the society. In larger democracies the state finds it difficult to manage the society when globalisation brings a negative impact on the society. But both the market and the state thrive on the support of the society. For both success and failure the state and the market should own responsibility as there is a strong connection between the state and the market. It is a fundamental question whether society regulates or influences the market and the state or *vice versa*. If we accept the proposition that the state and the market regulate the society and not the other way about, we cannot justify the liberation of social groups from the clutches of the dominant class and societies could not have been liberated from the colonial yoke.

Societies react, respond and act according to their level of understanding and commitment. The level of reaction varies from society to society. In this context everyone turns towards the society to mobilize the people to react to the market and the state. Intellectuals have been working with the state and the market as it is rewarding financially and otherwise also. In democratic countries people try to mend the state by which market can be well regulated through the state for the benefit of the poor. It is not an easy process. Working with the people is not easy. People are not in one group or segment. People are at difficult levels in terms of perception, attitude, behaviour and understanding. Globalization has lifted the economic, political and administrative activities beyond the reach of the common man[4]. Governance, administration and other decision making processes have been made simple for the advantage of the market. The same governance and administration are not so simple and easy at the grassroots[5]. They are made complicated and mystified. The poor cannot understand the process of governance and administration. In order to empower the rich for quick economic activities, all the barriers in the governance and administrative processes have been removed and governance and administration are simplified, whereas, in the case of the grassroots, governance and administration are not simplified and, instead, they are complicated and mystified. By doing so the people are driven from the mainstream to the periphery. All economic activities have driven the people from the rural to the urban areas. People's migration from the rural to the urban areas is for securing their livelihood[6]. The market forces draw the people towards consumerism. In India 77 per cent of the people are not in the purview of the new economic activities. They are far away from the development framework of the country. Of the farmers in India 84 per cent are small and marginal farmers. They have nothing to contribute to the economy. Hence 75 per cent of the people need the special attention of the state. The small and cottage industries, are able to provide employment opportunities and produce marketable commodities for the internal market. This segment is able to help the economy. But they are not attended to.

As a result people in the rural areas are kept an on-lookers or consumers and beyond that there is no advantage for the people in the rural areas. Thus rural life has been made miserable. It is not only in India but also in the West and North America[7]. While migrating to urban areas, towns and cities are made venerable. Against this background one has to think what could be done for the poor, marginalized and oppressed in the rural areas. Political parties and pressure groups are mobilizing them politically and they are being engaged politically but they are not engaged for development. As a committed citizen what can one do from the professional point of view? As academics, the leaders in the University system can do a lot more for the rural society apart from educating students coming from the rural areas. The issues that the rural communities confront at present require much deeper research as they are highly complicated because of globalisation[8]. Unfortunately, well qualified scholars with a sense of commitment are not many in the university system at present to do such investigation on the issues of globalisation. Academics have the main role of teaching and research in conventional universities and teaching, research and outreach programmes in rural universities. Knowledge creation, knowledge dissemination and human resource development are the major responsibilities assigned to the teachers of the universities. Yet they have a major role in influencing the society by initiating direct and indirect contact with the society. Teachers have social responsibility beyond preparing students. How teachers have to intervene in the affairs of the community and society and in the same way in the decision making and policy making domain have to be seen perspectively.

Rural Realities[9]

The character of the rural society has undergone a sea change and now we find only a mixture of global and local characters. Today the villages have roads so that even a remote village can be reached by road. Bus services are available to reach even the remotest places through mini bus services. Hiring of taxi, owning of motor bike, wearing of watches and cooling glass, using cell phone, cococola, mineral water, wearing jeans, chudidar, midi and nighty are accepted practices and youths are aspiring to get all these things. Previously people used to go to markets but not the market reaches the people wherever they are. In every house, whether it is big or a small or hut, one will find a television set with electric connection free of cost.

Every Gram Panchayat provides water supply to the habitats but all the small water bodies owned by the communities are abandoned. All water bodies are vested with different agencies like Public Works Department, Agricultural Department, Agriculture Engineering Department, Social Forestry Department and so on. As and when the departments get funds, they will desilt and strengthen the bunds. Otherwise all the water bodies will be abandoned. Water bodies were created by the communities in the past. But now, to desilt and strengthen the bund the government gets World Bank loans.

Vast stretches of lands are lying waste. Farmers have abandoned farming as agricultural labourers are not available in the village as they are going for National Employment Guarantee Act Scheme activities. Further farmers argue that getting credit is difficult. Even if they get credit, it is at high interest rates. Further the vagaries of the monsoon play a major role in the life of the farmers. The total support system for farmers was dismantled long back. Now the government gives only relief to the defeated farmers. Despite all those difficulties the farmers cultivate lands. Even if they get some output from agriculture, the prices are not commensurate with the input. Farmers argue that industrialists get credit at a lower rate of interest, produce products and fix the price for their articles. But the farmers have no control over anything. The price of their products is determined by the government. So the farmers are leaving agriculture. Farmers are willing to sell their lands for real estate or for company farming. The tiny marginal and small farmers are moving out from agriculture. This is the rural scenario today.

Throughout the day the liquor shop is busy in sales. Irrespective of the age group, people consume alcohol. 80 per cent of the people in the villages have got into the practice of consuming alcohol. Society has been spoiled by fixing the target of alcohol sale through the shop run by the state government. As a result, in a small village, there are 260 young widows struggling for their livelihood because their husbands are the victims of alcohol. One can find large number of young widows among the fisher folk in the coastal areas. Whatever money is being earned by men and women in the villages is being spent heavily on liquor, cosmetics and commuting.

Many artisans have lost their jobs as their skills have not fetched them jobs. For instance, village carpenters have relied on agriculture for preparing implements for farming and repairing the same. As farmers have begin to rely on tractor and other machines for farming operations, the carpenters cannot find jobs. Moreover the tools which are being used by them are obsolete and not usable for production of fine furniture for the market. So they have lost their jobs. As a result they have lost their skills. Carpenters, goldsmiths, blacksmiths, potters, people who are involved in mat weaving and a few other jobs are not relevant at present. As a result they are going for NREGA work at present. Previously we had skilled workers but now their skills have no relevance and hence they are unskilled. Since agriculture has become non-profitable and unviable the farmers have sold the bulls, bullock carts and even the animals meant for manure yielding. For their small farming operations they hire tractors. Only the milch animals are being reared and milking is done only at places where the vendor takes the milk for sale.

Young men and women, both educated and uneducated, who developed an aspiration to achieve development have picked up some skills and they have gone to foreign countries to earn. Since globalisation has provided enough opportunity for expansion of construction industries, these youth found jobs in the Middle East, Singapore and Malaysia. In the same way they have migrated to West and North America. Some of them have got some work in the nearby towns and they go for the job regularly and earn their livelihood.

Even in a small hut one can find a television set provided by the government in addition to a metal stove with gas connection. In some of the houses one will find fans, a grinder and even a fridge as they are all being supplied at cheap rates payable in instalments. Used articles are also sold in the market. For the electricity connection they need not pay as it is given under single light scheme free of cost.

Every one knows that it is a single light scheme but now it has become multipoint electricity connection. But nobody raises any question about this misuse as it is a state-wide phenomenon. Poor women form SHGs save money and use it for their betterment. They have been oriented in credit management by which they have escaped from the traditional moneylender and usury.

Village porompokes (common land) are meant for public utility. Now they are being encroached upon by some vested interests and since they belong to the ruling political party no one raises any question. Once the same land was used for grazing purposes. Common lands were used for fuelwood growing and were used by the poor for fuelwood collection. Now everything has gone. As a result the poor are also purchasing fuelwood. Poor families used to rear animals and birds as they fetch some income for their family. These animals can be reared by using the common grazing land. The poor can collect fuelwood from the common lands. But now they have all disappeared.

In every village the Dalits are residing in the outskirts. One will find water supply connection to the Dalit hamlet but water will not come as it is distance from the water sources. Normally water sources are in the place where dominant communities live. All the wastes of the village will be dumped in the areas where the Dalits are living, which are always in low lying areas. During the rainy season, the entire habitat becomes a waterlogged place unsuitable for living. Yet they live on in the same place. The Government provides houses to the homeless of the Dalit communities. They are owning the houses given to them. But the beneficiaries are not involved in any of the activities in the house construction. They occupy the houses all of a sudden. They develop a perception that the houses are given only by the government and hence they need not take any interest in owning the responsibility of managing the house.

In every village in every street there will be a temple constructed by the community for each and every caste. In none of the temples Dalits are permitted to enter. How are these temples constructed? With the help of the politicians and the contribution of the community they are constructed. Every year they collect money from the people and celebrate the temple festivals. Huge amounts of money are spent on this. It is a pride for the villagers to celebrate the temple festivals. In every school there is a Balwadi or Anganwadi to take care of the pre-school children. The conditions are pathetic. They do not have adequate facilities and they are not in a good sanitary and environmental condition. There are primary schools without facilities and attractiveness. As a result eligible children are getting admission in private schools. There is a sub-health centre in the same conditions. For a cluster of villages, there is a primary health centre with all facilities. Yet the poor do not rely on it but they go to private hospitals. The poor are also paying education tax and yet they are sending their wards to private schools by paying money. For educating their children the poor are making double payment. In the same way, the poor are paying from their hard earned money for health expenditure.

In many villages the traditional panchayats are dominant and they are entrusted with the responsibility of managing the commons. The traditional panchayats settle minor disputes in the villages. The commons are to be managed by the constitutional panchayats. But, in villages, traditional panchayats pay some nominal amount to the constitutional panchayats and the income generated from the commons will be kept with the traditional panchayats. In many panchayats the constitutional panchayat leaders develop conflict with the traditional panchayat leaders over the management of the commons.

All village stores are selling all packed food items and all kinds of beverages including bottled water. All kinds of cosmetics are available in the village stores. But the local varieties of beverages are disappearing. People who are in the government jobs and those who are in other slots for earning have constructed pucca terraced houses. Of course, they have availed of loans from the banks. These new houses which they have constructed are having toilets and they are being used. In all other places, barring a few houses, still open air defecation is in practice. In many places toilets have been constructed but they are not in use.

The school is yet another symbol of the village. Since free bus passes have been given to all school going children, by using this option, students are opting for private schools in the nearby towns. The primary schools of the panchayats are functioning without adequate teachers and adequate facilities. Parents who are not having any idea about their children's educational plan send their wards to such public schools. The schools are managed neither by the panchayats nor by the public. They are being managed by the bureaucracy. As a result it becomes a symbol of the village and beyond that it has no significant role. People are periodically mobilized by the political parties for protest marches and support marches and thereby they earn their livelihood also. They are paid for it. Sometimes one wonders if political parties are the biggest agencies to generate employment opportunity for the people in the rural areas.

In no way has the status of women improved despite the educational opportunity provided to women. Female literacy has increased. Yet the educated women have gone home and not entered the public domain. The brilliant girls are disappearing from the public domain as they get married and continue to remain in domestic chairs. Only a few girls who are under compulsion to earn and save their family continue in the public domain.

The struggle of women for emancipation starts from the womb and ends in the tomb. Even to be born they have to struggle. The perception of men about women has not been changed progressively. Because of modernization external appearance has changed. One segment of women have come to the public domain and they are in struggle. Life and living conditions are not conducive to lead a happy creative life in the rural areas. They are always driven from the rural areas to urban areas for want of employment opportunity. This kind of migration has intensified the process of urbanization. Now India has become a fast unbarnising country. Still 73 per cent of the people are living in the rural areas. In India some states are urban states and some districts are urban districts.

Further the strong control of the government departments over the people has further made them worse. People are made beneficiaries of government schemes and programmes. They have been lured towards the schemes and programmes for which people should get patronage either from the party—mostly ruling—or the officials. People do not have the wherewithal to claim their entitlements. Though they submit petitions to claim their entitlements, their submission is not as citizens but as submissive petitioners. After the establishment of the New Panchayati Raj System, all development activities are reached through the development brokers. They are party men, mostly from the ruling party. All individual benefits can be claimed only through the brokers. In such a way a scientific corrupt system has been systematically developed.

The local panchayats, which are to take responsibility for governance, are groping in the dark and always go by the order of the officials. Actually the officials are ruling the people. The panchayats are performing the role of a contractor and beyond that the villages are not under their governance. Even to perform the due role, the panchayat leaders expect guidance from someone. Neither the leaders of panchayats nor the leaders of the community are aware of the nuances of governance and administration. Both are mystified in the villages. Even the concept of development is not clearly spelt out. People believe that development is nothing but increasing the wealth status. People do not understand the meaning of well-being and human development. People are not aware that Indian Parliamentary Democracy stands on the support of the rural masses. They only elect the government by their votes. But they always feel helpless and they feel that they are only beneficiaries and petitioners. They never think that they can claim their entitlements as rights. Rural masses never entertain the habit of claiming their rights as they have been given a perception that they are at the receiving end as beneficiaries. They feel that they are the people placed at the lowest lawyer in the hierarchy of governance and society. 73 per cent of the people are living in the rural areas and they decide the destiny of governance in each and every election. The poor are solid in participating in the electoral process. Despite their contribution to Indian democracy, the Indian State has not done solidly and substantially by improving the living conditions of the people in the rural areas. Governments continue to spend the resources on various aspects of rural life but not on the needs and aspirations of the people.

Of course, the Centre and the State will give statistical details about the allocation of money to the rural areas. But the question is whether the allocated money has reached the villages. It is not so. This is the statement of the Prime Minister of India. The late Rajiv Gandhi said this in the Parliament himself. It is the reply of the Central Government also. In order to make the allocation work, a responsive, responsible and representative governance institution is created in every village. By inducting women and Dalits into the body, panchayats truly have been made inclusive institution of governance. But they are not allowed to function by the dominant elite class and the bureaucracy.

Donor agencies are coming to serve the poor and to alleviate poverty with a grant and loan. Despite their attempts, the expected results have not been achieved. Finally, it has been summed up that people are mobilized politically, socially and culturally but not economically. There is no development engagement in the rural areas by involving the people. They are working for their livelihood. People are in struggle but they cannot emerge successful.

To sum up, the rural areas have not improved to the level expected in terms of living conditions and standards even after sixty years of democratic governance and implementing plenty of schemes and programmes of rural development by investing huge resources of the people. Apparently some of the infrastructural facilities have improved. In terms of human development there is no marked improvement. Livelihood has been totally disturbed. Agriculture has been made non-profitable. As a result people who relied on agriculture have to find some suitable alternative option. They migrate to urban areas to seek employment. The money they fetch by their hard work has to be spent on liquor, cosmetics, travels, cultural activities, wards' school education, medical expenses and so on. Even social relationship has not improved as untouchability is still in practice. Conflict erupts in villages. Dalits are not able to live harmoniously with other communities. It is always a communal tension in the rural areas whenever the Dalits are not permitted to enter the temples by the other dominant communities. In many places some of the clever politicians have found a solution by giving money to the Dalits to construct their own temple. Villages are not in the framework of the provisions of the Constitution but they are under the provisions of the community constitution.

What has to be Done?

To change this syndrome what has to be done at the micro level and at the macro level? Who will take the initiative? With what strategy? The development of a society or a community depends on the synergetic work of many. The government is a major player. Civil society is a support structure and catalyst. Equally the academic and intellectual community has to play a role. Where and how can academics play their role legitimately for the benefit of the society? Academics can contribute in the world of knowledge by creating knowledge. By disseminating the created knowledge to bring about change in the society academics can contribute substantially. By sensitizing the policy makers and decision makers through policy advocacy policy modifications can be achieved. Academics can work on the above areas. By working with a community, citizens can be created with civility and communities can be empowered. By supporting the governing institutions at the grassroots by giving needed input good governance can be achieved. What we want at this juncture is connectivity between the academic world and the rural society. A formal linkage has to be created through an institution by which continuous outreach programmes can be conducted in the rural areas. Moreover students can be exposed to the rural reality and it will be a worthy experience for them. Learning is deepened only through action and participation in real life situations. By doing this kind of experiment the whole mode of teaching will be changed to learning which is more effective for the students. Thus enormous opportunities are available for both the academic communities and the rural communities to work together for the benefit of both. This connectivity will enable both to work in a "win-win" situation. First a linkage has to be established. Of course, at present such a kind of linkage has been created in two kinds of institutions. They are agricultural institutions which have a formal linkage with the community through their extension wing or department. In the same way Rural Development Institutions are also having such a kind of connectivity through the Department of Extension. They have been doing such kind of activities for long but they could not make inroads. Much impact has not been created both theoretically and practically as their activities are isolated. When this kind of linkage and activities are created between technical institutions and industry, it will create an everlasting impact.

Role of Academic Institutions

In this context one has to evaluate the activities of the social science departments and institutions in terms of knowledge creation and knowledge dissemination about rural realities. No doubt academics have intensively studied the rural societies. Scholars from different traditions with different approaches have conducted studies with different aims and objectives. There are a large number of empirical studies carried out on rural population and services delivered in the rural areas. Equally another set of studies have been carried out theoretically on social group relations and the culture of the rural communities. In the same way studies have been carried out for the purpose of planning and policy initiatives on human settlements and on the rural population. There are other aspects which are covered in three major domains. The following subjects were taken up for analysis empirically, theoretically and policy and planning perspective: Population, Social groups, rural service delivery, human settlements and culture[10].

Table 4.1: Concentration of Studies on Major Areas

Sl. No.	*Subjects*	*Empirical*	*Theoretical*	*Planning Policy*
1.	Population			
2.	Social groups			
3.	Rural services			
4.	Human settlements			
5.	Culture			
6.	Livelihood			
7.	Economy			

– Large number of studies – Less number of studies

There are a few scholarly traditions involved in the analysis of rural issues. They are positivist and qualitative, hermeneutical, Marxist, feminist and post-modern and structuralist. All the traditions have focused attention on the context in which the rural society lives, the philosophical foundations of their life and activities and the existing practice of social institutions and reality. They are presented in the following table for easy understanding.

The whole analysis has focused on certain major areas, namely population structure, social needs, class structure, economic activity, caste structure, cultural activities, political mobilization and gender disparity. Though they made such analysis with different knowledge traditions with different approaches and frameworks, they could not move beyond the conclusion. All their contributions are laudable and they are being used for teaching and research. Yet the conclusions, way forward and suggestions remain static as suggestions and are not put into practice. Academics have not moved beyond teaching and research. To change the scenario academics have to move towards outreach activities. Potentials are vast and they can be utilised not only for the benefit of the society but also to enhance the skill capacity of the academics. By establishing contact with society through

Table 4.2: Types of Traditions and the Analysis

Sl. No.	*Tradition*	*Contextual*	*Philosophical*	*Practice and social ---*
1.	Positivist and qualitative	Economic development, Modernization, Industrialization, Agriculture	Evolving generic pattern models Evolving variables for prediction	Observation, measurement, objective documentation
2.	Hermeneutical	Dissatisfied with qualitative approaches – real life stories	Real life experience recording symbols values identifies deeper implications	Indepth observation, social practice, deeper meaning Recording everyday life
3.	Marxist	Widespread protest unrest mobilization movement	Critiquing capitalism Impact of capitalism in rural life challenge inequalities	Mode of production Social and economic relationship
4.	Feminist	Gender disparity and women liberation	Status and position of women incorporating women experience of patriarchy	Challenge to unequal status of women – women narration – case studies
5.	Post-modern and post-structuralist	Importance of cultural altributes pressure to pressure and conserve	Deconstruct the key concepts – Role of language	Commitment to deconstruct dominant narratives diversity of rural life.

outreach programmes academics can be alive, active, vibrant, up-to date, and relevant and useful and even evolving.

With regard to policy advocacy and mobilizing people in the rural areas, the civil society organizations have played a major role. Yet they are inadequate. India needs more effective, committed and scientific outreach action by the academics to transform the life of the poor, women and Dalits in the rural areas. In the Indian context, there cannot be one model applicable to the whole of India. India has different regions and one does not concur with another. Within regions there are sub-regions. Within each sub-region one will find variations because of the caste, culture, community practices. Hence approaches need to be changed and newer methodological nuances have to be adopted suitable to the region and the people. Primarily the problems of the rural areas have to be identified. Secondly, policies and programmes of the government, both Centre and the State, have to be identified contextually. Further resource allocations for rural development have to be assessed and the track has to be followed. The flow of resource has to be identified and tracked. Steps have to be taken to match the needs with the resources of the government. To make the resource work profitably what steps have to be taken has to be assessed. In all the domains academics can help.

First problems in the rural areas have to be identified. They are: (a) shrinking livelihood options, (b) disappearing rural skills and knowledge, (c) fast depleting natural resources, (d) crisis in agriculture, (e) living conditions of the poor and the marginalized, (f) natural disasters, (g) large scale migration for want of employment opportunities, (h) mounting waste in the rural areas, (i) people's poor understanding of governance, development and administration, (j) poor health conditions of children and mothers. All the above issues are drawn from fieldwork done in Tamil Nadu for a period of five years[11]. In this context, it is necessary to go back to history and remember what M.K. Gandhi explained in his constructive programme. They are: (a) Communal unity, (b) Removal of Untouchability, (c) Prohibition, (d) Khadi, (e) Village Industries, (f) Village Sanitation, (g) Basic Education, (h) Adult Education, (i) Women, (j) Evaluation in Health and Hygiene, (k) Provincial Languages, (l) National Language, (m) Economic Equality, (n) Kisans, (o) Labour, (p) Adivasis, (q) Lepers, (r) Students. On all fronts we could have done substantially but we have not done so. As a result we are facing a chaotic and deplorable condition in our society.

To change the existing situation what role the academics can play is discussed in the following pages. To address the above issues, how can academics, through their institution, bring about development in the rural areas? The activities can be generated through the concerned departments by following certain strategies. When we talk about the role of academics in the society it implies that the activities are done directly as an outreach programme. There is yet another activity that implies equipping agencies, organizations and institutions to perform their role and responsibilities professionally in the rural areas.

Framework for Extension Activities

One has to remember that the outreach programmes framed and implemented by the Agriculture division of all the universities have not made a significant impact. As a result farmers have committed suicide and agriculture has gone into the background. It is not able to contribute to the economic growth of this country. Yet 60 per cent of the people's livelihood is totally relying on agriculture. No doubt 84 per cent of the farmers are marginal and small and their productivity is low. Hence they are always in debt. To help meaningfully the people

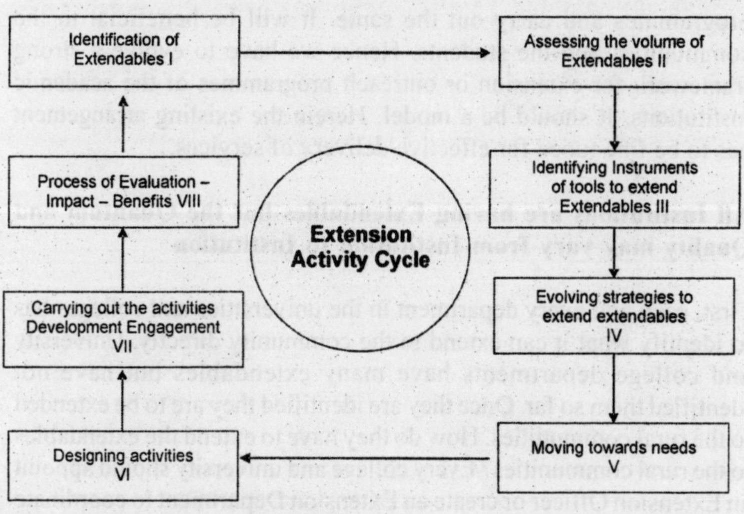

Diagram 4.1: Framework of Extension Activity Cycle

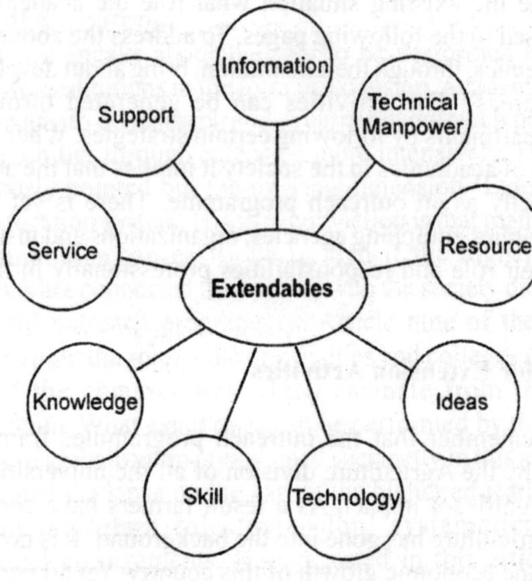

Diagram 4.2: Menu of Extendables Available in the Academic Institutions

in the rural areas for their betterment academic institutions can design programmes and carry out the same. It will be beneficial to the communities and the students. Hence we have to evolve a strong framework for extension or outreach programmes of the academic institutions. It should be a model. Herein the existing arrangement has to be fine tuned for effective delivery of services.

All Institutions are having Extendables but the Quantum and Quality may vary from Institution to Institution

First, each and every department in the universities and colleges has to identify what it can extend to the community directly. University and college departments have many extendables but have not identified them so far. Once they are identified they are to be extended to the rural communities. How do they have to extend the extendables to the rural communities? Every college and university should appoint an Extension Officer or create an Extension Department to coordinate the activities of different departments professionally, depending on the volume of extendables. In some colleges and universities huge volumes of extendables may be available and, in that case, a department is necessary for transmitting the extendables from the educational institutions to the community. In some academic institutions there may not be much of extendables and hence an Extension Officer is enough for the whole institution to conduct outreach programmes for the purpose of extending the extendables.

The extension or outreach programmes and activities have to be carried out professionally. They are to be done in a systematic way. Hence it is necessary that the areas where they are going to work have to be identified. It may be a geographical area or a segment of the society. Whatever activity is carried out, it should be need based and then only it will create an impact.

Secondly, the whole programme has to be formulated with the basic objective of enabling the students to gain learning experience from the work that they carry out in the community. Both the teacher and the taught can narrow down the gap between the book view and the field view. All intricate rural problems can be conceptualized by periodical visits of the students to the rural areas. There are certain institutions which cannot work directly with the communities but they can help the communities by enhancing the skills and capabilities of the institutions, individuals and groups working with people. In the same way they can work for enhancing the skill and capabilities of the rural development leaders and functionaries.

When finalising the strategies one has to keep the basic principles in the backdrop. Extension and outreach programmes cannot be done on a charity basis. In sixty years of freedom, the development works done by both the government and the civil society organizations have left the people with an indelible mark. People are recipients or beneficiaries and hence they are not treated as respected citizens. People who receive benefits treat themselves as secondary citizens. Agencies which are involved in development activities have not developed perspectives. As a result the concept of charity works in the development domain. That is why it is strongly argued that development is the right of the people and not the charity of the government.

Further strategies have to be evolved and thereby all the activities have to be carried out in the communities. As the activities are impact making in nature they are to be designed professionally and effective strategies have to be evolved. All the activities have to be designed in such a way that they meet the specific needs of the communities.

Focusing on certain geographical locations, extension activities can be carried out effectively. Constant and continuous work in the community will keep the people engaged in development. The local institutions both formal and informal, can be involved in the development engagement of the people.

The whole development engagement of the people done through the outreach programmes has to be assessed and evaluated scientifically. By evolving certain parameters the activities are to be evaluated and the advantages and drawbacks have to be identified. Two key aspects have to be considered for evaluation. One is the impact created by the extension activities and the other is the impact created in the students in terms of their learning. Primarily the learning impact of students are more important than the other. Further it should not be donor driven. No work should be done in the community unless we have the resource. It should be based on the needs of the community and it should be expressed by them. In the same way it should not be top down but it should be bottom up. These are non-negotiable points in carrying out outreach or extension activities.

There should be a template for easy and scientific evaluation of extension work carried out in the communities.

Table 4.3: Framework to Evaluate the Extension Activities

Sl. No.	*Expected outcome*	*Activity*	*Method*	*Outcome*	
				Students	*Community*

In the whole process of evaluation the main weaknesses in the activities and methods have to be identified and they are to be recorded and they are to be removed. Departments can be grouped to attack the issues in the rural areas. Technical input can be given by the staff and students of the technology departments. Input to create awareness and capacity building can be provided by the staff and students of Social Science Departments. To tackle energy and environmental issues in the rural areas, technical input can be given by the Science Departments through their staff and students. For all technical input to farmers, the faculty and the students of the Agriculture College or

Department can help. In the same way medical students and staff can help the Panchayats to assess the health status of women and children. The Department of Adult Education and Legal Departments can help the village Panchayat to achieve literacy and legal literacy. These are all illustrative activities identified, based on the existing practice in many of the institutions in India.

Table 4.4: Menu of Activities

Facilities and Departments can be Grouped to Reach Out to the Communities for the Following Activities:
• Awareness can be created among the people about the new Panchayati Raj System and the importance of the Gram Sabha. • Awareness can be created among the people about the duties and responsibilities of the citizens. • In every village a citizens' centre can be created and the centre can be activated as a debating centre, discourse centre, information centre and discussion centre. • In every Gram Panchayat administrative area, basic data can be collected and maintained in the Panchayat office. • As per the Biodiversity Act, in every Gram Panchayat a biodiversity register has to be maintained with the details of the flora and the fauna. • People can be mobilized for the Gram Sabha meeting and facilitate the effective conduct of the Gram Sabha meeting. • Water supply in every Gram Panchayat can be streamlined. Needed awareness can be created among the people about water literacy. Technical input can be given to Gram Panchayats for proper distribution, the quality of water and the level of the stakeholders' need. • A perspective development plan has to be prepared for every Gram Panchayat with the active participation of the people. In the plan, the needs of the community can be matched with the schemes introduced by both State and Central Governments for rural development. • All the children in the villages can be screened medically by which the health status of the children can be assessed. • All the women aged between 21 and 50 could be medically screened and the health status of the women in the Panchayat area can be assessed. • Computer literacy can be created among the school-going children. • Computer literacy can be created among the SHG members. • An energy audit can be made in every village and thereby energy saving devices can be introduced to the Panchayat functionaries. • Alternative energy resources have to be utilized for energy requirements. • Awareness about clean healthy habits can be created among the people. • Building the capacity of the Local Body Leaders can be done. • Capacity building can be done for the officials working at the grassroots. • All rural development innovative practices developed and practiced elsewhere can be documented and disseminated.

- Rural development practices workshops and conferences can be organized periodically
- Rural Development magazines can be published and circulated among the Gram Panchayat leaders for proper dissemination among the people during the Gram Sabha meeting.
- Skill upgradation training can be organized for skilled persons in every village with the help of the community or technical institutions.
- For every village a natural resource development and management plan can be created.
- Enabling the farmers to reach out to the exact market to get remunerative prices can be done.
- Farmers can be assisted technically in farm operations.
- Gram Panchayats can be assisted to prepare a labour budget and the surplus labour can be diverted to the needy places through on line transaction.

Conclusion

By carrying out well planned, scientifically designed outreach programmes both the students and the communities will gain benefits. It is a win-win situation for students and the community. It is a win-win situation for teachers and the students. By doing extension programmes the gap between the field view and the book view will be narrowed down. Teachers, with the help of the students can collect data and the same can be used for the projects and their field knowledge will be enhanced by this kind of outreach programmes. People's living conditions will be changed. Needed awareness can be created among the rural folk on the aspects of development, democracy, governance and administration. Then they will be able to understand the Human Development aspects. Secondly, they will understand the process of governance and administration. As a result they will be in a position to claim their entitlement. Local body leaders' capacity can be enhanced. Skills of the people can be enhanced. Productivity of skilled persons will be increased. By adding small technological inputs, service delivery will be improved. By assisting the Gram Panchayats in collecting basic data from the Panchayat area and consolidating the same, a scientific data base on all basic details about the village can be created and maintained in the Gram Panchayat office. Infrastructure for economic activities can be created. Scientific data can be generated from the villages and they can be updated. Micro plan can be formulated for each and every Gram Panchayat. While creating the micro plan, people can be sensitized on the vision of their village, the vision of their family and their life. By building vision, people will work for the development of the community and the village. People will be enabled to demand their entitlements, not as charity but as right. Capacity of the bureaucracy who serve at the grassroots can be enhanced. There is no professionalism among the grassroots bureaucracy and, as a result, their service delivery work is poor. By building the capacity of the grassroots bureaucracy, the system can be improved.

By carrying out all these activities, the capacity of the teachers and the students will be increased. The existing conditions in the rural areas need a lot of input from external agencies for development. People in the rural areas need awareness, information, skill upgradation, credit, infrastructure, marketing facility and so on. The officials who are working with the community at the grassroots do not have the needed capacity to tackle the problems of the rural society. The leaders who are in position in the local bodies do not have the understanding and the skill needed to perform their role and responsibilities. For total transformation of the rural society, the government thinks that rural development schemes are sufficient. But along with schemes some more input is needed. The market argues that privatization of public services will transform the rural areas. Now, it has been that proved that both the state and the market have failed. In this context, it has been argued that a people centric, participatory, community driven, bottom up process of development programme alone will transform the rural areas.

Notes and References

1. Joseph Stiglitz, *Globalisation and its Discontents,* New Delhi: Penguin Books, 2003.
2. Joseph Stiglitz, *Making Globalisation Works,* New York: Allen Lane, 2006.
3. Ranjita Mohanty and Rajesh Tandon (eds.) *Participatory Citizenship: Identity, Exclusion and Inclusion,* New Delhi: Sage Publications, 2006.
4. G. Palanithurai and R. Ramesh, *Globalisation and Rural Development,* New Delhi: Concept Publishing Company Pvt. Ltd., 2008.
5. G. Palanithurai, "Governance and Administration Reform at Grassroots", *Public Administration,* Vol. 4: No. 4 (October, 2008).

6. Ruedi Baumgartner and Ruedi Hogger, (eds.) *In Search of Sustainable Livelihood Systems Managing Resources and Change,* New Delhi: Sage Publications, 2004.
7. Roger Epp and Dave Whitson, (eds.) *Writing off the Rural West: Globalisation Governments and the Transformations of Rural Communities.* Edmonton: University of Alberta Press and Parkland Institute, 2001. pp. 89-108.
8. Madhu Purnima Kishowar, *Deepening Democracy: Challenges of Governance and Globalisation in India,* New Delhi: Oxford University Press, 2005.
9. The Issues and Problems projected here are drawn from the reports prepared by the students of Gandhigram Rural University after their village placement programme every year. The students have to stay in the rural areas for a week in every semester and prepare report based on their observations and analysis. It reflects only the conditions of Tamil Nadu.
10. Paul Cloke, Terry Marsden and Partrick H. Mooney (eds.) *Handbook of Rural Studies,* New Delhi: Sage Publications, 2006.
11. From the Financial support of the Ford Foundation rural issues are analysed in the backdrop of Globalisation. The reports are:

    G. Palanithurai, R. Ramesh, *Actionable Learning Handbook for Local Self-government*, Gandhigram: Rajiv Gandhi Chair for Panchayati Raj Studies, 2007.

    G. Palanithurai, *Globalization: Concerns at the grassroots and how to address them?* Gandhigram: Rajiv Gandhi Chair for Panchayati Raj Studies, 2007.

    G. Palanithurai, *Managing Globalization—A Guidebook for Panchayats,* Gandhigram: Rajiv Gandhi Chair for Panchayati Raj Studies, 2008.

    G. Palanithurai, *Report of the National Workshop for validating the research studies on Globalization and Decentralization 7-9 August 2006.* Gandhigram: Rajiv Gandhi Chair for Panchayati Raj Studies, 2006.

5

We Can Also Do It!

Recently I had an opportunity to visit the University of Lethbridge, Canada, under the auspices of the Shastri-Indo Canadian Institute and I was in the University for a month with Prof. Trevor W. Harrison of the Sociology Department. While I was working with him in his room, I saw a small newsletter entitled *the Post* published by the Parkland Institute of the University of Alberta. While going through the newsletter, I found an interesting area where the Parkland had made a mark—that is, linking the academic institution with the larger society, which made me visit this institute. It is not a very big institute. It is only a name taken by a group of academics, doctors and lawyers by contributing their time to evaluate the activities, performance, policies, programmes, and budgets of the governments periodically, particularly the Government of Alberta, and informing the public through *the Post* and interacting with the media to generate a debate over the issues which they project through their research. The activist group gets funding from the public and the funds are managed through Alberta University. The university provides a working space for this group. From the funds raised, they pay the salary of the researchers and the administrators. Periodically they organize conferences to shape public opinion based on the informed opinion and observation put forth by scientists and academics. The key problems faced by the Alberta province are taken for analysis and they bring out reports, submitting them to the government for policy consideration. They submit the same reports to political parties and members of the Legislative Assembly to raise the issues in the provincial Legislative Assembly. In this way political science teachers have taken a lead in linking themselves with the larger society apart from teaching and research. When senior professors do not adequately concentrate on teaching, they are substituted by newly recruited teachers and for them the salary is given from the project as the senior teachers give their time to the project. But this institute, to maintain its independence, has made it a mandate that it should not get funds from the government and corporate companies. Last year, they managed to raise resources to the tune of Rs. 1,43,17,880. Individuals give donations annually and monthly. This institute does not get money from the university also excepting for its annual convention up to 1250 dollars. Issues which affect the life of the people, especially the poor, are taken for analysis and reports are prepared and they are placed before the public. In this way they have developed commendable professionalism. The university gets a name because of the activities of the Parkland Institute. Society gets valuable information to make correct choices and raise its voice to correct the approach of the government.

The purpose of bringing this information here is to raise a question as to why and in what respect we are incompetent to do the same. I am not saying that no university is doing this kind of work in India. There are, indeed, a few exceptions. India is a vast country. Every state can have such an institute to analyze politics, political behaviour, governance, administration, programmes, policies, money allocation and so on and link itself with the larger society. At present there is no active linkage between academia and the larger society. Our academics are not worthless. They are also sound but there is no voluntarism and innovation. They just need to form a team and meet periodically to discuss issues of governance, development, democracy and administration. Our teachers write articles and books, present papers in conferences but they do not connect themselves to the community and the larger society.

If they come together in today's context, no university is going to say no to such a kind of research and policy advocacy on many of the live issues. One can collect any volume of criticism against the prevailing polity. But what kind of politics do we want in this country, where are we to get opinion and to whom shall we offer the opinion and how? A creative minority has to do this. It does not mean that they have to join politics and purify politics. By creating public opinion we can purify politics. By way of suggesting reforms, we can purify politics. All politicians are not bad. There are honest politicians in each and every political party. However, for good politicians, there is no support in the party system. By extending needed support to the good politicians, politics can be purified. It is a well known fact that in South Asian politics families dominate provincial and national politics. It is a trend in this area. Hence, politicians coming from an impressive family tradition can be shaped properly, trained and oriented, for which a new group of political science teachers can work. For all these activities what is needed is a commitment on the part of political science and public administration teachers and researchers. Along with commitment they require professionalism with a high degree of integrity and probity. Normally in the Indian context such kind of teachers do not have a habit of working in a team. Team work is the need of the hour, which is called partnership. If a team is formed with qualified teachers with a research bent of mind, no university will say no to the proposal of creating a small centre with some title such as Parkland Institute in the University of Alberta, because all the activities of the small centre will be carried out through the university. The university will get name and resources. This kind of activities will help the students and researchers to gain much experience in the new process. An active action research culture will be cultivated. Students will be involved in intensive research activities on the critical issues affecting the community and the society. The public will get needed information and opinion from this research group for their reaction to public policies and programmes. The Government will also get feedback. Political parties will get well researched information for their political activities. In India, such a kind of work will attract the government departments also and hence we can get funds from the government also. Many State Governments and Central Government Departments are looking for such active research groups for policy and programme analysis. These are all possible in our country. What we have to do is to give a worthy name for the critical work to be undertaken. To make it happen professionalism is the need of the hour and integrity is the key factor. Our pessimists will say that this kind of activities are possible in countries like Canada and the USA or in some of the Western countries, but not in our country as our universities are predominantly under the control of clerks who are well trained in the ways of the erstwhile colonial administration and the Vice-Chancellors and Registrars who are under the clutches of these clerks in the name of rules and procedures. Moving beyond this framework one has to have control over Syndicate politics. To overcome all these hurdles, one needs honesty, goal and team work.

Here is a case in our own university system. The Rajiv Gandhi Chair for Panchayati Raj Studies in Gandhigram Rural University (*which was not created by the HRD Ministry, Government of India*) was created one decade back with a group of academics in Gandhigram Rural University to activate grassroots democracy after the enactment of the 73rd Amendment to the Constitution of India. It was a purely voluntary work. It created awareness among the people about the new dispensation in the villages in collaboration with NGOs who were wedded to the cause of Rural Development. It got assistance from the NGOs to print pamphlets and organize meetings. Having seen these activities, the Rajiv Gandhi Foundation provided some financial assistance to appoint a professor in the Chair for a period of three years. The UGC gave financial assistance to recruit two research associates for the Rajiv Gandhi Chair. Subsequently a campaign was started to exert pressure on the State Government to enact conformity legislation. To activate the campaign, an NGO network was created, which was called 'Tamil Nadu Campaign for Panchayati Raj'. After the enactment of the legislation a workshop was organized to review the entire legislation and it came out with a document for appropriate modification and change in the State Panchayati Raj Act. Further, to make the State Government conduct the elections to local bodies, the Rajiv Gandhi Chair organized a series of programmes and of them one major campaign/programme was conducted throughout the state for which many NGOs helped. Finally, it had to lobby with many political parties to include "conduct of Local Body Elections" as a major promise in their manifesto as they had to face the elections in 1996. The party which promised to conduct local body elections came to power and conducted the elections. Even in the electoral process, the Rajiv Gandhi Chair participated by creating voter awareness among the people. After the elections, the Chair started a capacity building exercise for the Local Body Leaders. For the capacity building exercises the Government of India and the Government of Tamil Nadu extended financial support. Training modules and manuals were prepared and validated and distributed among the NGOs to conduct such exercises in their respective areas. For the women leaders and Dalit leaders who were in need of special training this was also arranged and conducted by the Chair. The women leaders and Dalit leaders, even after the training, expected handhold support when they faced problem while discharging their roles and responsibilities. Hence a support structure was created with a team of experts to help them to work. The women leaders and Dalit leaders were federated to address their issues on their own. The Hunger Project, New Delhi, and the Ford Foundation helped to do all these specialized activities. Periodically the leaders were taken to other states and other districts for interface. The Dalit and women leaders were also enabled to organize regional and state level conferences to address their issues. To disseminate information about the New Panchayati Raj System in Tamil Nadu to the public and Panchayat leaders, the Rajiv Gandhi Chair entered into an agreement with a vernacular daily newspaper to publish a special supplement every Monday for Panchayats under the title 'Panchayat Malar'. One page was reserved for Panchayat news. In the same way, the Chair entered into an agreement with All India Radio to broadcast a programme every Monday to reach out to the masses under the title "Good Governance through Local Governance". The above programmes were supported by the Hunger Project, New Delhi. In the meanwhile success stories and struggles in Panchayats were captured, analysed and documented for dissemination. The media is a key player in any democracy. Hence the Chair wanted to sensitize the media on grassroots democracy and so it conducted a series of workshops in different parts of Tamil Nadu for media persons.

To develop micro plans in villages the Chair helped the Gram Panchayats to collect data and analyse the same through the Participatory Rural Appraisal method. Model plans were developed in seventy four Gram Panchayats in five districts with the active cooperation of the District Administration. These Panchayats serve as models for other Panchayats. For almost all Panchayat activities the chair has emerged as a powerful research and capacity building agency. Both the Central Government and the State Government nominate academics from the Chair as members of task forces or working groups in the Planning Commission. Commissioned studies have been undertaken for the State Finance Commission by the Chair. The Chair has built up its research capacity and, as a result, it has undertaken many studies for donor agencies also. Recently the Chair has completed a project on "Globalisation and Decentralisation" for the Ford Foundation. A newsletter titled *Global and Local* is being published periodically. Under this project, eight sectors have been studied empirically and the reports have been published. Panchayat leaders have been trained to understand the process of globalisation and decentralization and they are oriented to make use of the opportunity which they feel come from globalisation and to avoid threats, if any, coming from globalisation. Instead of discussing globalisation metaphorically and anecdotally, the Chair has demonstrated empirically the implications of globalisation and the opportunity made available by decentralization to respond to globalisation.

For the World Bank project on "Empowerment and Poverty Reduction" in the State of Tamil Nadu, the Rajiv Gandhi Chair serves as a capacity building agency. It trains the cadre of project leaders who are going to work in the rural areas on this project. When the Tsunạmi struck the coastal areas of Tamil Nadu, the Rajiv Gandhi Chair worked with 17 Gram Panchayats to evolve a micro plan to reconstruct the devastated villages with the support of the SDC and the Hunger Project, New Delhi. It was essentially building the community and the Panchayat's capability to manage disasters by being prepared. Based on this experience, the Chair organized several workshops to evolve a disaster code and a disaster management policy for the State of Tamil Nadu.

In order to sensitise academics on the issues of grassroots democracy, four refresher courses of 21 days' duration have been organised for college and university teachers and subsequently the Chair undertook to revise the syllabus of the courses in "Local Bodies in India" and "Local Bodies in Tamil Nadu" and sent the same to Tamil Nadu universities for adoption.

Currently, apart from conducting capacity building exercises, the Chair has undertaken a study for the Ministry of Panchayati Raj on "Tracking Panchayati Raj Finance in Orissa, Andhra Pradesh and Tamil Nadu" and another study for Action Aid on "Role of Community and Panchayats in Disaster Management". The Chair is currently involved in preparing a District Human Development Report for two districts, namely, Dindigul and Nagapattinam, for the UNDP. Thus the Chair has drawn the attention of many regional, national and international institutions and organizations by its continuous work in the domain of Panchayat Raj. It has 24 vibrant young researchers and fieldworkers working for it. It has prepared separate administrative manuals for Panchayat leaders and officials and published the same.

Because of all these activities of the Chair, Gandhigram Rural University gains name and recognition; its staff members gain name;

the society gets benefits; many researchers are trained; the Department of Political Science and Development Administration gets substantial infrastructural facilities; and research scholars obtain valuable research documents from the Chair. Now the Chair is the pride of this university. It started from mere commitment. The University has given no money but it has extended support and facilities and it has gained monetarily and in popularity. For NAAC accreditation, it gained lots of points for research, extension and consultancy. So it is possible in the Indian context also.

I commenced this article from my Canadian experience because our people believe something if it happens in foreign countries. To show a model I have explained the activities of the Rajiv Gandhi Chair. The Chair was not given by the UGC but created on the basis of a shared commitment. It survives on its performance. There is no permanent funding for the Rajiv Gandhi Chair of this university. A committed team can work and it is possible in India also. By doing so, it can achieve what kind of polity and quality of polity we want. The need is commitment on the part of the academics.

6

Role of Teachers in Higher Education System

Higher learning institutions have to play an important role in any society for its higher level activities. It has three main functions namely teaching, research and outreach activities. All the three functions are entirely depending on the commitment and capability of the teachers. If the commitment is ensured and capability of teachers is enhanced with the best efforts of the institutions the individual teachers output of the institutions is always high. Efforts of the institutions and individual teachers are essential for the smooth and efficient functioning of the institutions. Yet individual teacher's efforts are more important even in shaping the character of the institutions. More specifically in India, in a hierarchical society the teacher's role in higher learning institutions is crucial and critical in achieving material prosperity and social equity and equality through the three functions of the teachers. How an ideal teacher will perform the three roles effectively and efficiently in the higher learning institutions are explained hereunder:

I

A teacher in a higher learning institution is an open learner. He or she is learning continuously for the sake of co-learners who are the students. The teachers have to make the students to learn consciously. Further, he or she has to teach learning methodology to the students. The students have to be put in learning mode. To be in learning process students have to learn the methodology of learning. Methodology of learning has to be taught to the students and thereby the students have to be placed internally in themselves and to be made to stand on their own in learning. The learning process should be enjoyable and it should give confidence to them that they are in a process and journey to move from known to unknown. In such a way learning methodology has to be taught to the students by the teachers.

The learning must be an open minded and it should not be dogmatic and ideology oriented. Further it should be critical and creative. To perform the above, students should have communication ability. In the course of building the communication skill, deliberative skill of the students have to be imparted consciously. Students have to be ably assisted by the teachers to pick up the skill to think creatively, critically, analytically and comprehensively. Students should not stick to attitude and they should change the attitude and in such a way the students have to keep themselves. Hence, they have to learn the art of changing attitude. In a hierarchical society, students coming to higher learning institutions from different strata of the society are with different disabilities. Students who are coming from the lower segments of the society will find difficulty in learning. In such a situation their difficulty has to be properly understood and the teachers should have sympathy for them. They should also feel the learning process more enjoyable and joyful. In such a way teachers have to enable them in the learning process.

II

A good teacher should always be a good researcher. A teacher in higher learning institution should always be a good researcher. Because knowledge creation, knowledge updation and knowledge dissemination are the prime functions of the higher learning institutions. Unless the teacher becomes a researcher, one cannot expect the students to travel in research corridors. A teacher in higher learning institution is a specialist. He or she has to work continuously on the chosen areas and build knowledge on the specialized area. He or she enjoys in teaching only when he or she transmits his/her research findings. In the same way he/she finds joy in teaching. Without being a good researcher, he or she cannot be a good teacher. If anybody claims that he is a good teacher but not a researcher, he is to be considered as only a tape recorder. A teacher, who is always a researcher, has to continuously publish papers, books, working papers, monographs, and articles. An ideal teacher consciously lives on his area of specialization and by which he/she makes a tradition. A teacher has to go to larger audience through his ideas, concepts, approaches and frameworks. He should be either in foundational research or in contemporary contextual and relevant social research. Either way he/she should be in research. Only a good researcher can enthuse students by his creative ideas. A good researcher is enabling the larger society to move forward in its activities by his innovations and creations through his research. The same teacher is enabling the humanity to reduce its conflict through research. It is to be understood that the human society is advancing by its higher level activities only through continuous research. Thus research is part of the teaching in higher learning institution and without which teaching is incomplete.

III

Yet another role, apart from teaching and research has to be performed by every teacher in higher learning institutions is outreach activities. Extension or outreach is the third dimension of higher learning institutions. It is nothing but connecting themselves with larger society by the teachers. The teachers in higher learning institutions have several extendables and they are to be extended to the larger society. The extendables may be in the form of ideas, skills, knowledge, and services. Even teaching is also an extension. In every higher learning institution an array of extendables are available and they are to be extended to the society through appropriate strategies and approaches. By doing so the communities are getting benefits directly from the knowledge society. As a result social transformations could be made faster and society will move for higher level of activities without much barriers and difficulties. Hence, every teacher is an extension worker. Thus he/ she is closer to the communities. Thus a teacher in higher learning institution has three main roles to be performed consciously and by doing this job transformative process is activated fastly.

7

An Ideal Department in Higher Learning Institutions

We have departments, centres, schools and faculties in higher learning institutions in India. Coordinators, heads, deans, chair persons are the leaders of those units. Whether it is a centre or a department, or a school or a faculty, they are mere governance, administrative and coordinating units to get the best out of the stakeholders who are working in these units. Activities of governance, administration and coordination of these units are being judged by the outcome of these units. In terms of quantity and quality how these units are achieving their outcomes in terms of producing students through teaching, research and outreach activities is a major question. All the three kinds of activities are interrelated and mutually dependent on each other for bringing out fine quality outputs. How to achieve this task is the major work of the institutional leaders and the leaders of the departments, schools and centres. It requires vision, commitment, strategy and action on the part of the leaders. The institutional and unit leaders have only limited time frame as these positions are tenurial and within which they have to create a culture for quality work in the institutions. A department or a centre or a school, has first to free from factionalism. Harmony and congenial atmosphere have to prevail in the institution for best quality work. In most of the units, the leaders have to concentrate more on resolving crises and problems created out of factionalism among the teachers working in higher learning institutions. While admitting students for programmes up to Ph.D merit should be the primary consideration. At the same time the students who hail from the marginalized communities should also be taken and they should be given utmost care to bring them up to the level of the expected standard of the department. Despite many such provisions are created by the University Grants Commission, the teachers have not involved themselves in this process of building up the skill level of the students coming from the marginalized students. Every department should have a specialization and all the faculty members should have partnership in the specialization process. When quality recruitment is done for the department, every one will find academic pride in his/her specialization. A department is constantly adding new knowledge to the subject in which faculty members specialize. All the teachers should contribute through their continuous research publication and by which the department should be made known to the country and abroad. Mobility of the teachers by attending serious kind of seminars, workshops and conferences depending on the contributions made by the teachers. Ceremonial mobility will no way add new knowledge to the subject or discipline.

Periodically seminars, workshops, symposia and conferences have to be organized on the areas of their specialization. Every faculty members should have projects. It may be pure research or action research. By doing projects, faculty members can facilitate himself or herself by adding needed facilities to her/his research and contribute for infrastructure facilities of the department. Many of the departments have equipped infrastructurally because of the project culture they have developed over a period of time.

Every department should have the research council or research circle for periodical interactions among the faculty members and researchers based on their research activities. Students have to be involved in all the academic activities apart from attending their mandatory academic programmes. Students can be used for data collection while they go to the field work. The data can be used for writing article, monograph and working papers. The department should be made dynamic with full of activities in all the three dimensions namely—teaching, research and outreach. The department should be known nationally and internationally through its unique academic programme, research publications and outreach activities. The faculty members should reach out to larger audience through their research and extension activities. Quality culture should be maintained rigorously in teaching, research and outreach activities. The staff members should continuously interact with National and International level institutions. Unrestricted mobility for the teaching staff will enable them to reach out to larger audience for their equipment and disseminate their findings. In such a way faculty members have to be facilitated.

Faculty members have to publish, based on both foundational and socially relevant research projects, articles in referred journals, monographs, working papers and books. Apart from the above, popular articles can also be written to reach out to the masses. Annually special lecture programmes can be arranged for the students by inviting eminent persons based on the need and requirement. While conducting academic programmes research and outreach institutional norms have to be followed. The minor irritation among the staff could be solved internally. In such a way a harmonious relationship has to be maintained among the staff in the department. By its functions, it has to draw the attention of the student community, researchers, funding agencies, government institutions, and the media. Experts and academics should feel proud if they get invitation from the department. The students passing out from the department should find adequate job opportunity. Their certificates should carry much weight because of the department and teachers wherefrom the degree is obtained by the students. Government institutions and larger society should feel that the utility of the department is valuable for the society. In such way the department should build its capacity, capability and skill.

To achieve the above, leadership of the department is crucial. In any organization or institution people will work for external goods and internal goods. Leadership of the department through his/her vision and commitment should put up himself and herself as model for others in teaching, research and outreach activities. The staff should be motivated and facilitated to carve out a place in the department through his/her specialization. Every one should feel comfortable and safe under the leadership. The leadership should concentrate on the system, processes and procedure development rather than personality development. The department should stand on the system, process, procedures and culture established there rather than the personality who is in the helm of affairs. The leader of the department should be a visionary and he/she is always facilitating and enabling the staff to move in the career ladder. The leader of the department should have high moral authority and stature.

Thus the development of any department in higher learning institution depends on many factors and of which the leadership of the department and the institution is crucial and critical. Their vision, commitment and strategies will play vital role in shaping academic, research and outreach culture of the departments.

8

Education System of Germany: Special Focus on Higher Education

I was in Germany for about six months and I worked in Cologne University in the Indology Department and the centre for Modern Indian Studies. I offered four courses namely Indian Society, Indian Rural Local Governance, Contemporary Critical Development issues in India, and Education and Business in India. In the course of six months I had interaction with Faculty members, researchers, students and citizens of different segments. I have visited universities, vocational schools, business establishments, trade centres, chambers, villages, local government offices, civil society organizations. I make observations and comments on the functioning of the Higher Education System in Germany based on the above process.

Introduction

Education system in Germany is much complicated as education is totally in the hands of the provincial governments and as a result one will find wide variations among the provinces. At present the education system is undergoing a total transformation required to meet the contextual need of Germany and the world. It is moving towards Globalization, Europeanization and Provincialisation. The education system of Germany has been geared up to meet the International standards, European standards, National standards and retaining the provincial uniqueness as education is the subject of the province in terms of decision-making. Yet one aspect of education in Germany VET system is more important which draws the attention of not only the European Countries but of the whole world. Vocational Education and Training (VET) is the most attractive aspect of the education system of Germany which is well regulated and managed by both the German Federal Government and the provincial governments despite there are certain shortcomings and difficulties. India can draw some inspiration from it and experiment the same to transform the unskilled youth into skilled and resourceful youth needed to the job market. The Germany VET system has got tremendous potentials to produce the skilled manpower required to the market and reduce the unemployment rate. By this system substantially our youth can be engaged in development. The present condition of keeping the unemployed youth as dole receiving beneficiary can be changed into employable youth of the country.

There is yet another reason for writing this article. The Government of India has recently signed a Memorandum of Understanding with Government of Germany for helping educational institutions in India to implement the Vocational Education and Training as it is practiced in Germany. In this context the Minister for Human Resource Development has requested the Indian universities to make use of the opportunities to sign MoU with leading institutions in Germany for such a help to build the skill of the students. Against this background I have gone into the details of the system and interacted with many people who are on the job in Vocational Education and Training and visited many schools. Apart from the above I interacted with many who got Vocational Education and Training. It is to be underlined here that the impact of VET system is reflected in professionalization of human activities in every walk of life in Germany. Whether to burn the dead bodies to clean the platform in Railway station, professional training is needed and a certification by the recognized institution is needed. Thus every action is done in the society professionally.

Box 8.1: Professionalism

Every summer there used to be a festival in Koln Reine River. On a particular day during the night there will be a fire work activities in the above place. Different kinds of crackers have to be burnt. To see the light of the burning crackers several thousands of people will be on the two sides of the river. Even in the river there will be mechanized boats in which hundreds of people will be seated. From 11.30 to 12.15 the crackers have to be burnt. While burning the crackers, there will be music. It has historic significance. People used to throng the two sides of the river to witness the colour lights of crackers which they are burnt. While burning the crackers, one could notice the synchronization of the music, tunes and the colour design of the crackers while burning. The sound will always be mild and matches to music also. The whole exercise was done in a boat in the river. It was really a thrilling exercise. It was telecasted live with lot of fun and explanation. After seeing the whole exercise when I asked many, they told me that the whole cracker burning was done by a team of skilled workers who were trained for this purpose. Unless there is a certificate no one is allowed to do that job. So every action bearer of a small bar to star hotel, certification is needed and without which no one can do the job. In such a way human life has been professionalized in Germany.

Objectives of the Vocational Education and Training System (VET)

In order to achieve social cohesion and harmony, prepare a skillful cadre of workforce for the industry, make the youth more resourceful to earn decent earning and to make the productive sector more competitive, the Vocational Education and Training system has been developed in Germany. It is not the sole responsibility of the educational institutions to conduct the VET system in Germany. It is the collective responsibility of the stakeholders. Before the secondary education Germany has pre-primary and primary education.

Primarily nursery is made optional but primary education is compulsory from the age of 6 to 11 or 12. The system of education varies from state to state as education is the subject of the province. States decide their own educational policies. Secondary education of Germany has five types of schools. German children only attend school in the morning. Homework will be given to the students by giving importance to three "R"s and only a very few extracurricular activities.

Children who have completed primary education have to be admitted in secondary education. It was considered as a crucial period of the development of the children. There are four options in secondary education. The students are admitted in different streams based on their ability and capability. The students have options to choose. Hauptschule is one such type of secondary schooling where least academic tasks are being transacted. Until grade nine these students were not given much load. There is yet another type called Realschule which is carried out upto tenth grade. It is almost an exit point. The third type is Gymnasium (Grammar School). It is meant for university education. To qualify oneself to go to university education an examination has to be taken by the students. The examination is called Abitur. The fourth type is called Gesamtschule (Comprehensive School).

Table 8.1: Overview of the German School System

Sl. No	*Grade Level*	*Age*	*School level of Berlin and Brandenburg*	*School level rest of Germany*
1.	1	6/7	Primary Education	Primary
2.	2	7/8		
3.	3	8/9		
4.	4	9/10		
5.	5	10/11		
6.	6	11/12		
7.	7	12/13	Secondary Part I	Secondary Part II
8.	8	13/14		
9.	9	14/15		
10.	10	15/16		
11.	11	16/17	Secondary Part II	Secondary Part II
12.	12	17/18		
13.	13	18/19		

Source: Computed.

The whole secondary system is designed in such a way that the students who have successfully completed in any of the above schools can start a career with an apprenticeship in the Berufsschule (Vocational School). The vocational school is normally attended twice a week during a two, three or three and half year's duration, and on other days the students have to work in the companies. It is with an objective of providing students knowledge of theory and practice. During the apprenticeship, the apprentice is a part time salaried employee. After the successful completion of the apprenticeship through an exit exam, the students are ready for a career upto a low management level. For certain specialization, students after taking the exit examination, have to register themselves in appropriate bodies like German Bar Association.

Provincial governments are responsible for education and professional education. The federal government can influence the educational system only by providing funds. In Germany there are many different school systems. For the students grades five and six are really an orientation phase and in this phase teachers, parents and students have to decide which of the paths the students have to choose has to be decided. In this process the teacher's recommendation plays a crucial role in deciding the path. Teachers make recommendation for the students based on the scholastic achievements and attitudinal and behavioural traits in the classroom. Further the recommendation should be made suitable to the legal requirements of the provinces also. Teacher's responsibilities for evaluating the student's performance are crucial in the educational systems of Germany. It is not one general type of education they provide. It is a universal truth that all children are not having uniformly the same capability. The students have to be classified and based on their evaluation they have to be sent to different schemes of education. In Germany the teachers whether they are in schools or colleges or universities they are professionals, fully devoted to the profession. The system of education is constantly supervised by the stakeholders. All the time the teachers have to devote their time for their profession. If we compare Germany with India, our teachers in India either in school education or higher learning institution are not professionals devoted to the profession barring a few institutions.

Higher Learning Institutions

Students who want to pursue higher education have to clear Abitur examination which is final examination of the school system. It is to be noted that the students who are completing the school system are somehow equipped for a career. Going to higher education depends on their capacity and the choice. It is criticized that student's abilities for their career are evaluated only at the tender age. One cannot judge the ability of an individual at a tender age. But suitably reply is also given for this question. Nobody is prevented from coming to university education. At any stage even if the students are in vocational stream can come to higher education through clearing an examination of Abitur. If a student is evaluated in the secondary level and classified him or her for suitability at a later stage by their performance and he or she can join in higher education. Absolutely higher education is not free for all. It requires higher mental ability and accordingly students are filled through Abitur examination. When they are evaluated at a secondary level school many might not have mental ability but later they acquired such ability. In this context, it is necessary that the students have to be clear that Abitur examination. Once a student clears Abitur he or she is eligible to get admission to higher learning institutions. Here one has to understand the higher education system of Germany. In the name of increasing the enrolment of students for higher education, they are not allowing students who are not having requisite capability to pursue higher education to the portals of higher learning institutions. Germany provides opportunity to all to come to higher education provided the students have got the requisite capability. In this process the quality of higher education is maintained and they stand competitively in the world of education. The quality of man power production is intact.

Language Learning Capacity

English learning is compulsory throughout in secondary schools. Students in Academic stream should learn Latin as their first foreign language. In some of the states, foreign language education starts in the primary school. French, Spanish, ancient Greek and Latin are more frequently taken as the second and third foreign language. Many schools also offer voluntary study groups for the learning of other languages.

It is interesting to note that the Governments are encouraging the students to learn more languages and particularly the languages of the Western Europe with the primary objective of free mobility in the West European countries. This process of learning foreign languages has enabled the students to learn any language at any stage very easily. From this perspective one could see the language learning capacity of the students of the West European countries. In India politicians are the biggest stumbling block for enabling our students to learn more languages. Additional languages are the source of empowerment and it will enable the students to migrate to other provinces and countries. Migration brought wealth to families, groups, regions and nations.

Education for Children with Special Needs

There are different types of schools available for children with different needs as students are having different disabilities. They suffer from learning difficulties, severe learning difficulties and children with special emotional needs. One in twenty one German children attends special schools meant for special needs. All the special schools are with qualified teachers trained to look after special needs children. Though it is needed it is being criticized that this kind of special needs schools discriminate students from other students. It is also true that all the students who are with different disabilities are not joining the schools created for the special needs children.

There is yet another system of schooling in Germany. There are very few specialist schools for intellectually gifted children. They perform very well in all their studies and they go for higher studies. Many reports and studies reflect that these children are having high self esteem and maintain good psychological health. It is also being criticized that a new class is being created within an equal society. Because in the regular stream itself they find opportunity to go up in the ladder.

Strong Foundation

German education system had a strong foundation starting from 12th century. A free and compulsory primary education was introduced in 18th century. It consisted of an eight year course of basic education. It provided not only the reading, writing and arithmetic skills but also the basic values for leading decent human life. They are ethics, duties responsibilities, discipline and obedience. In the beginning the Germany's education system was influenced by the Lutheran advocacy. Martin Luther had advocated compulsory schooling in order to enable the people to read Bible independently and interpret the same. Hence, this advocacy had a great impact in the education system of Germany. The centralized school system and the key role of the state in educational system were the foundational aspects of German Education system. The classification of school system had originated from the formation of German Empire itself. The state established its right over the school system of the entire empire. It continued further up to till date.

Affirmative Actions

It is true that people with migrant background are affected in the evaluation process in the educational institutions for taking the students for higher education. Next to migrants the working classes is yet another section affected by this evaluation process. It is to be noted here that the students are classified to different streams not because of their socio-economic background or because of the biased evaluation process. The students are evaluated scientifically and there is no bias in their evaluation. But the reality made the people to think why migrant's children or children of the working class could not go for higher studies large in number. Even there is a provision for free and compulsory primary education, large number of families of migrant origin has not sent their wards to schools. This problem was solved by a scheme of home visits to families in need and by which all the parents are personally met by the trained professionals. It is not only for orienting them to send their wards to schools but also to orient the mothers to change their attitude and behaviours to increase the performance of their children. Families whose children are performing below average or poor in academic activities are visited by trained professionals. They offer variety of services to them depending on their needs based on their background. It is a kind of counseling to the pregnant women of low income families. In the course of their visits to these families the women are given tips about the changing behaviour of the pregnant women and changing performance of their kids in education when they are in school. In order to get a healthy baby for higher performance in education, the professionals used to give advice to the pregnant women on healthy diet refraining from use of alcohol, use of tobacco during pregnancy. The low income pregnant women are given information about the correlation between positive health related behaviour of the pregnant women and the performance of the children born out of healthy practices during pregnancy. In such a ways steps are being taken to help the poor income groups in Germany. It paid rich dividends. Yet problem persists. It is only the left political parties brought up the discussion about affirmative action. No doubt it is a possibility to help the working class children who did not do well in school to gain access to higher education. But it was argued by the teachers that it is a kind of disservice done to the working class families as they will find it difficult to compete with other meritorious students in the classroom activities. The disability will continue even up to their job. It is not only doing disservice to the working class family students but also to the entire academic system as it will weaken the education system itself. But somehow or other quota system has been created. Quotas have been created for single parent families (the current rate of diverse is 54%) and migrant families. The quota is very less.

There is yet another interesting aspect one can notice in Germany. Though there are different kinds of private schools as per the study conducted in 2006, it is noted that only 6 per cent of German children attended private schools. Because all German schools (public schools) are provided with needed facilities, and qualified professional teachers. All public schools are well equipped with facilities, needed infrastructure and with qualified teachers. Yet another interesting aspect of the German Education is that church and state are separated. Compulsory school prayers and attendance at religious services are made against the constitution. Even Christian cross was not allowed in classrooms. Once the cross was fixed in every classroom. This practice was banned to protect the religious freedom of the non – Christian students. Some of the provinces of Germany banned teachers from wearing head scarves.

German education system is unique historically compared to other European countries in its early segregation and classification of students to different streams of schools. Though it is being criticized, it is the strength of the whole education system and the society as the system makes education relevance to social needs and market needs.

There are variations in the school systems, programmes and learning process as education as a subject which is being left to state. Provincial governments are responsible for education but resource allocation is being done by the Federal Government. In every school one could notice the parents council, and students council and they are functional. The buildings are being looked after by the Local Bodies. Even in India one could notice the Parent Teacher Association. It is functional only at a limited level. But in Germany it is functional and more specifically it is professional.

There are certain newer aspects emerging in the education system of Germany contextually. In order to compete with other counties federal standard in quality of teaching has been introduced. They have started working in this direction after seeing the low international ranking in programme. Secondly theoretical content has been reduced and practical content has been increased in teaching training programme with an objective of preparing students to the market needs and social needs. Thirdly some of the subjects have been taught bilingually. Fourthly schools are allowed to conduct experiments in teaching styles in order to reach out to the students easily and effectively. Fifth, all schools are equipped with computers with an objective of creating a culture of computer and internet use even in the school itself. They have started standardizing the school system on par with other western counties by reducing the academic school years. This is specifically to meet the international system requirements. It will facilitate the students to move from Germany to other countries and attract other country students to Germany.

Yet another unique aspect in Germany is its crafts. Germany maintains its high standard in the education of crafts people. People from crafts family rarely attend higher education. Though they are crafts people they receive respect and value in German society. The whole system of crafts people education is embedded in the relationship between the master crafts man and the students. It is a kind of paternalistic relationship. The master craftsman has got the sole responsibility of teaching crafts and virtues of craftsman.

There is yet another interesting process is going on in Germany education system namely Bologna process. Bologna process was initiated in 1999 in the Italian university in the city of Bologna with the active participation of European states to reform the higher education system. Basically, this initiative is to establish internationally accepted degrees and to improve the quality of courses of study and enhance employability of the students passing out from higher learning institutions. Both the Federal Government and the State Governments along with higher educational institutions are deeply involved in the reform process for the past one decade. The whole reform processes are well within the framework of Bologna process of reform. Number of youth entering in higher educational institutions is increased steadily and yet the enrolment of students in higher educational institutions in Germany is lower than that of many other European nations. This lower enrolment rate of students in higher educational institutions is partly due to the dual education system. In German education system the students passing out from the schools are qualified to start a career whereas in other European counties they have to take at least a Bachelor degree to qualify themselves to start a career. Many jobs which do require a college degree in other countries require only a qualification from a school in Germany.

Quality Maintenance in Higher Education

Quality in higher education becomes a culture and habit of the Germany's education system. Its testing point is the social relevance of the system. Moreover, quality is one of the objectives of Bologna process. Germany along with other European countries have evolved a framework and by which they want to improve the process of preparing quality manpower needed their respective countries and to rest of the world. Hence, they first started the standardization process and by which the degrees, diplomas and certificates issued by the universities in Europe will be standardized. Secondly, they initiated and updated the process of quality enhancement as the requirement of the market is quality product. Thirdly, they took steps to increase the intake of students in higher learning institutions. In the whole process of transformation in higher learning institutions, quality is the non – negotiable issue.

In Germany's higher education system, students are admitted based on the merit cleared through Abitur examination. A student can go to higher education only by clearing the Abitur test. Students those who are having such an aptitude will alone go to the higher education system. There is no compromise on it. Thus, only serious players will reach higher learning institutions. No relaxation for increasing the enrolment rate in higher learning institutions.

In order to maintain quality, performances of the teachers are evaluated and the capacity of the teachers is enhanced. Students are asked to evaluate the performance of the teachers. The report will be in the website of the university. It is open and everybody's name will be in the report. By this process teachers are put in a competitive mode to build and keep their pride and image among the students. The courses and porgrammes are need based. They are students oriented and not teacher centric. Whatever subject is taught, it is contextualized. The teaching and learning process emphasize the importance of the participation of the students. It is always in learning mode.

In order to maintain standard and quality centre for higher education quality is established in every school. It is attached with a senior professor. Researchers are appointed in the centre to do all kinds of evaluation studies. The centre takes care of the junior staff and one senior professor will be for quality enhancement of the senior staff members. The whole evaluation process of the staff is being done in such a way that it is meant for both the teachers and the students. It is not for the penalizing or denigrating the teachers. It is meant for enhancing the quality of the performance of the teachers. In such a way the programme is designed. Absolute objectivity is designed in the evaluation process. The whole evaluation process is perceived positively by the teachers. Observations made by the centre for the performance of the teachers have been visualized by the teachers positively and they take series of steps to improve their quality of performance. The quality maintenance centre will help the teachers to build and improve the teaching skills primarily. For the junior staff recruited a fresh, basic training would be given. For the senior professors and other teachers periodical seminars will be organized and through which teachers are facilitated to reflect on their performance and to pluck the loose ends in their performance. In this process teaching assistants, tutorial student workers are provided with needed assistance to build their capacity. Assistance is provided to the stakeholders to improve their quality of material prepared for teaching, and quality of material prepared for publication. In all dimensions and in all academic activities the quality centre would provide necessary and needed input. Since the whole teaching is done in a learning mode, assistance is provided to teachers to lead a group, to keep the students in interaction mode and to prepare teaching materials by using power point presentation. Staff from the quality maintenance centre will visit the departments; classes, projects, peruse the publications of the staff and give their feedback. Quality maintenance centre will have camera and other equipments. The staff of the centre will make video graph of the whole proceedings of the class and that will be handed over to the concerned teachers in the form of DVD. The concerned teacher has to see the DVD and to make an assessment and observation. The same DVD will be given to some experts also for comments. The expert comments will also be given to the concerned teacher. After a gap of one or two years the same teachers classroom performance will be video graphed and the new DVD will be compared with the old performance. By which the individual teacher is conscientised on the process of enhancement of their teaching and research skill and capacity. Periodically discussion is being arranged within the school on the quality of teaching and research. The quality maintenance centre will facilitate the teacher to

(a) increase the sensitivity of the new roles assigned to them
(b) how to conduct tutorials?
(c) how to build perspectives?
(d) how to evolve a good course?
(e) make the human learning process interesting
(f) information processing in the mind
(g) improve teaching methods

(h) improve teaching material preparations
(i) how to lead discussion?
(j) how to communicate effectively?
(k) how to look at the output finally objectively?

The Evaluation Centre is not only working for improving the quality of teaching and research but also evaluating the utility of the courses and its rigour and impact. Viability and utility will be determined from these evaluations. Periodically, the evaluation reports are put in the website. The courses are evaluated periodically. Incentives are being given to the best teachers in terms of their performance. While allocating resources to the department-quality assessment report is considered. In the evaluation process constantly they are getting the feedback from the old students who are in different jobs. Apart from the above evaluation of the centers in the respective universities an overall evaluation and ranking are being done for the higher education system of Germany. Mostly, they are being done by the media. Though it is not considered seriously, quality culture has been created in the higher education system.

Serious Players

In the higher learning institutions in Germany, students are serious, sensitive, interactive, communicative, regular, punctual, open and objective and performing their roles and responsibilities. When they register for a course, they do it only after a serious thought and through a consultative process. Students have wider choices. When they register for a course, they seriously chose the course. Hence, their attention will be cent per cent in the course.

In the classroom their attention will be full. No deviation or distraction for them. They will come with a small laptop, a voice recorder, a subject file, a tearable writing pad, and different kinds of pen, pencil, highlighter, marker, eraser, and sharpner. In the classroom interactive process, the students will be active participants and not passive listener. If they are not getting the points in the discussion, they will raise their hands and ask the teachers to explain again.

Classrooms

Classrooms are provided with needed facilities such as furniture's, black and white boards, wall mounted LCD for power point presentation, audio system, internet connectivity, different kinds of charts, OHP machine, dust free chalks and markers. The utilization of the facilities depends on the teachers. Every teacher is given an official email address. The students will interact with the teachers only through the email address. Normally students come with preparation as the teachers are giving references adequately to the students well in advance. The interactive process is enjoyable.

Conclusion

Higher Education system in Germany is in different culture and environment. The educational system had been designed in such a way that it would meet societal and market requirements. Professionalism plays a key role in the whole process. It is in the learning mode. The examination system designed for students to reach higher education portals filters the non serious players. Hence, students coming to higher educational system are serious players. Quality is the hallmark of the higher learning institutions. The students have wider choices and teachers have enormous responsibilities to fulfill the choices. Quality manpower production is the basic objective with which the whole higher education system is geared up. The whole higher educational system is undergoing standardization, internationalization process. It is specifically oriented towards market and society.

PART II

Rural Universities and Extension Activities

9

Rural Universities in the Era of Globalization

Introduction

'Rural Higher Education' has been a neglected subject in the overall framework of Higher Education in India. There is another complaint that the educational system in India has not been concretely erected on Indian needs and ethos, which has ultimately affected the whole fabric of the Indian society[1]. It is beyond doubt that the concept and the creation of Rural Universities or Rural Institutes or Rural Higher Education Programmes are basically viewed from the perspective of 'Nai Talim' evolved by Mahatma Gandhi[2]. Normally the popular assumption is that Rural Higher Education is closely associated with 'Nai Talim' of Gandhi. But the establishment of Rural Higher Education Institutions need not necessarily be against the backdrop of 'Nai Talim'. Many institutions have been created after India attained independence to help the government in carrying out rural development programmes. They are not all based on 'Nai Talim'. These institutions have been conducting academic programmes and training programmes related to rural development activities not based on the 'Nai Talim'. Many such institutions are autonomous and they are in the civil society domain[3]. The main discussion in this article is on the institutions based on 'Nai Talim'.

In India, historically speaking, Rural Institutes were created based on the recommendations of three higher education commissions and committees.[4] The newly created Rural Institutes functioned with distinctive characteristics and with innovative programmes (Academic, Research and Outreach) for some time with the active involvement of Gandhians and Gandhian Institutions. Over a period of time the Rural Institutes established thus disappeared. But time and again the need for such institutions is reiterated and sporadic attempts have been made in this regard as problems arose in rural areas.[5] It is a paradox that on the one hand the established institutions became defunct and on the other the need for such institutions was emphasized and reemphasized. Hence it is necessary to investigate the genesis, the growth and the decay of Rural Institutes and to assess the need for such institutes at present. There is yet another issue to be discussed: whether a Rural University is the only institutional mechanism competent to tackle the issues of the rural communities. There is a need to decide what kind of Rural University is needed and how it is to be established. Also to be discussed in this article is the question of how the existing Rural Universities have to be fine-tuned to bring back the original characteristics of the Rural Institute so as to meet the requirements of the rural areas.

Historical Background

'Rural University' or 'Rural Institute' is fundamentally a concept (to be debated) which gained currency among the policy-makers and Gandhian academics for some time in India after the submission of the report of the University Education Commission under the chairmanship of Dr. Sarvapalli Radhakrishnan.[6] The Dr. Radhakrishnan Committee Report is one of the acclaimed reports in India in terms of its vision. In this report a chapter on 'Rural University' was incorporated. It was written by one of the commission members Dr. Arthor E. Morgan, the President of the Tennessee River Valley Authority in the USA. He visualized an ideal university suited to Indian ethos. It is yet another paradox that a foreigner was able to show us the way. In this chapter an argument was advanced that the existing universities, focused on cities and towns and not on villages and the whole educational system was devised to prepare personnel for Government jobs and not for social transformation. Morgan urged that India needed a different, distinct, independent institution to prepare cadre of leaders to bring about transformation in the Indian Rural Society.[7] For three years from the advent of independence it was only a concept in the making till Nanabhai Bhatt translated the idea of the Rural Institute into action in

1951 in Gujarat. In his preface to the booklet entitled "Gram Vidhyapith" he dwelt upon the foundation of the Rural University. According to him, the edifice of the Rural University should be built on 'Nai Talim', the basic principle enunciated by Gandhiji. Bhatt unequivocally stated that the existing university culture had not shaped the younger generation with character, humility, commitment, responsibility and spirituality which was necessary to reconstruct the Indian society. It was to be recognized that the dreams of the founding fathers would be realized not through a few government servants and a few development schemes of the government, but only by invoking and involving the masses, for which a cadre of leaders and volunteers with a sense of commitment and values was needed.

Morgan's chapter on Rural Institutes has eight sections. In the first section he explains the context in which 'Rural Institutes' are visualised. The conditions of the villages and the basic education programme are explained. Undoubtedly it is all based on the Gandhian framework of rural reconstruction. India being a primarily rural society, has to be reconstructed in such a manner that the development achieved should be sustainable. The whole vision was against the on-going development process of modernization, industrialization, and westernization. It was to be almost a turning point in history.

In the second section post-basic education is explained. The third section deals with rural industrialization. The fourth division explains the reconstruction of Indian villages. The fifth section is the core area which deals with the establishment of Rural Colleges and Universities. In this section the characteristics, the curriculum and the methodology are explained. The sixth section deals with the basic concerns of Rural Universities. What kind of management and administrative systems have to be developed to manage the rural educational institutions, is explained. The final section wraps up the whole argument. The whole chapter challenges Gandhian educationists to conceptualize new education programmes which are to be integrated with the entire education system and policies of the government. It is to be noted here that the mainstream education followed the model of the West. The British system of education had been adopted and was in vogue. For the new education system every aspect had to be worked out and integrated with the existing system so that it could be acceptable to policy makers for evolving policies and allocating resources for strengthening the new educational system. As per this chapter, if the new framework for establishment of Rural Higher Education

Institutions raised hopes among policy makers, the entire education system would be totally oriented towards the Gandhian framework. Unfortunately the Gandhian educationists did not concretize the new education system and hence the Western model picked up vigour as it was well within the existing framework of the development process of the world.

In 1954 the Government of India appointed a committee under the chairmanship of Dr. K.L. Shrimali to look into higher rural education and offer recommendations. The Committee submitted its report and suggested an umbrella institutional set up to coordinate the Rural Institutes' academic activities. Based on the recommendation of the Shrimali Committee the National Council for Rural Higher Education (NCRHE) was established in 1955. In the first phase the National Council for Rural Higher Education identified ten institutions called "Rural Institutes" which would be later developed into rural universities. The ten institutions were:

1. Shri Niketan (West Bengal)
2. Jamia Millia Islamia (New Delhi)
3. Mouni Vidhyapith (Gargoti, Kolhapur)
4. Shivaji Lok Vidyapith (Amravati)
5. Gandhigram (Madurai)
6. Vidyabhawan (Udaipur)
7. Ramakrishna Mission Vidyalaya (Coimbatore)
8. Lok Bharti (Sanosara, Saurashtra)
9. Toorki (Bihar)
10. Balwani Vidyapith (Bichpuri, Agra)

Within a short span of time the Rural Institutes faced a plethora of problems because they were not in the broader framework of the Indian education system. In 1958, the problems of the Rural Institutes were discussed in an international seminar at Bichpuri. The Rural Institutes could not move further in the existing framework as they were caught in the bureaucratic net and, as a result, the Rural Institutes faced innumerable hurdles. Having experienced turbulent weather, the Rural Institutes had decided to be merged with the traditional university system within fifteen years of their existence without creating much impact and they turned towards the Western mode of educational system by changing into constituent colleges of affiliated universities[8].

If an analysis is made as to why the Rural Institutes could not survive, one would meet with surprises. It is necessary to keep the basic objectives as referral points for evaluation. The objective was to create a cadre of Rural Development leaders and managers to tackle the problems of the rural communities. Programmes were to be offered not to seek employment opportunity in Government Departments. They would be real change agents to bring about rural transformation. But the main reason attributed for the failure was that the graduates who passed out of the Rural Institutes were not able to get admission to the traditional university system in Government Departments. From these arguments one can infer easily that the students admitted to the Rural Institutes were not moulded, motivated, oriented and trained towards the objectives of the Rural Institutes. The students who got admitted to the Rural Institutes were also having the same objective of seeking jobs in the government system as the students in the traditional educational institutions.

The Gandhigram Rural Institute was the only institute that continued as a Rural Institute and delivered what it ought to deliver to the rural masses at a limited level with the dedicated staff under the leadership of Dr. G. Ramachandran. The staff who worked in the Rural Institute could not get remuneration as their counterparts elsewhere and yet they served the institute with a sense of commitment. Despite all trials and tribulations it tried its best to retain the characteristics of the Rural Institute. At that point of time it was well appreciated. Hence the University Grants Commission granted it the status of a Deemed University. Even at that point, a distinct structure could have been created suitable to the Rural Institutes' objectives. Instead the Gandhigram Rural Institute opted to follow the model of the conventional universities. This prompted the Gandhigram Rural Institute to make a slow departure from the basic characteristics of the Rural Institute.

The courses offered in the beginning were changed by citing the reasons stated by earlier Rural Institutes and, gradually, barring a few, all the degrees up to the masters came to be modelled on those of the traditional universities. The appointment of the Vice-Chancellor has played a crucial role in deciding the fate of the Rural Institutes. On many occasions Vice-Chancellors were appointed without any Rural Institute background. They managed the institute to suit their own philosophy. As a result the institutions were caught in the dilemma of either to go back to a 'Rural Institute' character or transform into a conventional university which they really could not do. One has to understand the challenges for the Rural Institutes had to be faced by the leaders of the Institutes by their innovative and committed action. They needed the support of the Government. In this context it is necessary to recognize and assess the honest attempts made by different institutions.

Assessment of the First Phase

Rural Higher Education gained momentum in Gujarat by the setting up of Gram Vidyapiths. Lok Bharti, though it remained an inspiring concept, could not leap forward despite the attempts made continuously. Three Gram Vidyapiths were established in Gujarat. They were in Bahadurpur (Baroda District), Samoda (Mehsana District) and Vedchi (Surat District). A Gram Vidyapith Society was formed to strengthen the initiatives of these Vidyapiths. To further their activities the Gujarat State Basic Education Board was sought to be established to coordinate the activities of 'Nai Talim' right from primary to Rural Higher Education. The proposal for establishing the Board statutorily failed miserably. The Rural Institutes created with enthusiasm, commitment and sincerity were not projected with a positive message to the policy makers and the people that the new scheme of education would deliver the goods and solve the problems of the rural communities.

The students who passed out of these institutions faced many problems as they were from a totally different stream from the mainstream framework of Higher Education in India. Many students from the Rural Institutes who wanted to pursue higher studies found it difficult to get admission to the conventional universities. Many who tried to get government jobs by showing the degree obtained from Rural Institutes could not get them. This has been projected as a reason for the drifting away from the concept of the 'Rural Institute'. This has been projected as the failure of the Rural Institutes. The real issue, however, is that the Rural Institutes had not performed as they ought to. In the name of Rural Institutes they performed the job of a college affiliated to a conventional university. It is also a paradox that these Rural Institutes which were expected to perform the unique role of Rural Institutes were brought under the rubric of the UGC. The UGC pattern is different and totally opposite to the direction of the Rural Institutes. In order to get funds, the Rural Institutes had to adhere to the norms of the UGC and, as a result, the Rural Institute experiments were diluted. As a result, they could not register any visible impact. They could not improve sanitation or livelihood, protect rural industries, innovate appropriate technology, provide health facilities, literacy, and, work for social change. They existed as show pieces. Beyond a certain time they merged with the conventional institutions. The old institutions like the Gandhigram Rural Institute and the new ones like the Chitrakoot Institute struggled to survive as they did not have appreciate leadership excepting the Vice-Chancellors. They too were mere managers for three years to run the show. They could not improve the functioning substantially. They could not provide ideological leadership for the Rural Institute. But due to the liberal funding of the UGC, they improved the infrastructure and enabled the staff to improve their career. They could not come out with academic programmes which could foster skills needed for reconstructing the rural areas and transforming the rural landscape. Sometimes, to justify their distinctiveness, the Rural Institutes introduced courses and programmes with a rural bias but the students could not get gainful employment. Ultimately, the students, coming to the Rural Institutes were from the lowest level of performance in schools without very little motivation.

Rural Institutes are being viewed as non-profitable white elephants. Only students with a low academic profile and low motivation join the institutes. Further, the rural institutes are driven by the funding agencies to produce more number of students as do the colleges. This kind of drive completely pushes the Rural Institutes to move towards the traditional institutions of learning. Hence affiliating these Rural Institutes to the traditional university system was inevitable and imperative from the perspective of the students' future as they did not have the needed motivation and commitment to serve in the rural areas for rural reconstruction and transformation. Here one has to recognize and underline that Rural Institutes were created not to train students to get clerical positions in government offices. They were to become change agents in the rural areas. But, unfortunately, a perception was developed that the students who got degrees and diplomas have to go for higher studies or get employment opportunity in the government sector. When Rural Institutes were seen from that perspective, many felt that the students faced problems. Moreover, many wanted to move with the mainstream education rather than carve out a different path distinctively different from the mainstream educational system. Even the degrees and diplomas in Rural Institutes were designed to suit the requirements of the traditional colleges and universities. In the meanwhile, the schools preparing students through basic and post-basic education started disappearing. The Gandhian institutions which had supported the Rural Institutes declined in terms of their activities in the framework of Gandhiji. Thus the Rural Institutes gradually lost their original character, mandate, approach and activities. They were all merged or affiliated with the traditional university system. The freedom of Gandhian experiments was given the go-by. The Rural Institutes started functioning as a soft variant of the traditional colleges and universities. Thus the Rural University or Rural Institute began to fade away. Only a few institutions have survived with lot of problems. Thus, the face of the rural university has been changed and it has assumed the characteristics of a college or a miniature traditional university.

New Initiatives

The concept of 'Rural University' gained much prominence after the release of the New Education Policy in the year 1986. It states that the new pattern of the rural university will be consolidated on the lines of Mahatma Gandhi's revolutionary ideas on education so as to take up the challenges of micro planning at the grassroots for the transformation of the rural areas for which institutions and programmes of Gandhian basic education will be supported. The policy envisages that educational institutions and voluntary agencies which take up educational programmes based on the concept of correlation between socially useful productive work, social service and academic study will be encouraged. Why did the New Education Policy reemphasize the need for the Rural Institute? It has to be viewed in perspective. Rural problems are mounting enormously and poverty reduction has become a real challenge to the rural development departments. Against this background the Central Government needed professional institutions to tackle the issues in the rural areas. Whether it was water supply, or sanitation, or livelihood, or primary education or primary health, or waste management, or rural energy, or rural employment the government required nodal institutions to help the government take appropriate policy decisions and implement them to achieve the targeted outcome. For this they needed institutions. Against this background the New Education Policy emphasized the need for rural higher education institutions. A Programme of Action was drawn up by the Ministry entitled New Education Policy, 1986. It advocated:

(a) Consolidation of the existing rural universities;
(b) Reorganization of the Rural Institutes established as a part of schemes of rural higher education launched in the Second Five Year Plan;
(c) Encouraging other institutions to take up Rural Reconstruction;
(d) Strengthening Rural Development Educational Programmes in select institutions;
(e) Supporting the elementary, secondary and post basic institute based on 'Nai Talim';
(f) Strengthening the content of all these institutions with emphasis on science and technology; and,
(g) Setting up of National Rural Institutes Council to manage the affairs of Rural Institutes and Rural Universities.

Nothing moved beyond preparation of documents for about six years. This New Education Policy was modified in 1992 and, subsequently, based on the new recommendations, the National Council for Rural Institutions (NCRI) was established in 1995 at Hyderabad by the Government of India. It is a registered society fully funded by the Government of India.[9]

It is to be noted here that how the newly created NCRI was to function was underlined clearly in the inaugural speech of the then Prime Minister of India, P.V. Narasimha Rao, on 3rd December, 1995.[10] His whole argument was to contextualize the Rural Institutes: they have to create cadres to manage development programmes. The cadres coming out from Rural Institutes should not be job hunters but job creators. The Rural Universities have to act as catalysts to help the communities through ideas, knowledge, skills and technology. These institutions have to transform the unskilled individuals into skilled workers to meet the market needs. The village life situation has to be transformed by implementing the constructive programmes, the activities ranging from village sanitation, water supply, livelihood, literacy, skill upgradation, small industries, infrastructure, communication, credit system, Panchayats Act. The gap between the higher level government and the people has to be narrowed down. The Central Government evolves excellent policies, schemes and programmes. It allocates plenty of resources for rural development activities but they do not reach the field. The schemes and programmes evolved by the Central Government have to be implemented speedily and professionally for which the Rural Universities have to work continuously as facilitators. Appropriate technologies have to be developed in the Rural Institutes and they are to be disseminated and transferred to the communities. In China, two universities are helping rural artisans to prepare articles out of bamboo for export. In this way traditional universities are working in China to help the rural communities. The existing Rural Institutes in India have to rise to that level to lend their help to the rural community based on their experience. To evolve new technologies and to upgrade the skills needed by the market are the imperative tasks of the Rural Institutes. In this manner it was emphatically stressed, the Rurai Institutes are to be contextualized[11] in the market era.

The Rural Institutes have to act as a support base for rural communities to make use of the opportunities coming from economic globalization and, at the same time, if threats issue from globalization, they are to be tackled by the community through the new Panchayati Raj System. Such a kind of contextualization has to be done in all Rural Universities.[12] Communities have to be in touch with the Rural Institutes for their needs. Such an interface has to be created between the Rural Institutes and the communities. A new cadre has to be created to manage the rural development programmes. These Rural Institutes are to be integrated with the larger society by which needed skills, capacity, technology and idea input will be provided. It was with this vision that the NCRI was created and, through a few Rural Universities was expected to function vibrantly. But now the question is how are they functioning and what have they achieved? These questions have to be answered objectively and honestly.

Assessment of the Second Phase

It is necessary to assess to what extent the second attempt to establish Rural Institutes and Universities has taken shape and to what extent the old Rural Institutes have lived up to their objectives. To be very frank, Rural Institutes were started but they could not survive and they disappeared. Only a few institutes are surviving. The NCRI was created only to rejuvenate the existing institutions and to establish new ones too. Hence, the assessment has to cover the NCRI and the old Rural Institutes surviving until now. First, one has to understand that rural development activities are facilitated not only by the Rural Institutes but also by many agencies in this country. There are government training institutions, specialized research institutes of higher order, departments (e.g. Rural Development) in traditional universities, civil society organizations continuously working for rural development by training the stakeholders involved in rural development activities, both leaders and officials, preparing needed cadres for rural development, assisting field work or working as outsourcing units. They are not designated as rural academic bodies but they do work for rural transformation and rural reconstruction.

Even after sixty years of continuous rural development activities by several agencies with plenty of schemes and programmes and pumping of huge resources, we could not make a bold statement that conditions have been created in the rural areas to facilitate a decent human life with all basic facilities. It is self-evident from the point of view of human development. Despite our schemes, programmes and huge resources for rural development, we could not create much impact on human development. Where are we now, in the human development report? Our position in human resources development will reveal our real achievements and failures. Even smaller countries with less growth have gone up in human development. Ours is a huge country with vast differences and it has been managed centrally and not in a Decentralised fashion. Till now we have developed a perception among the people that 'development' is the work of the government and not of the community. People have developed a dependency syndrome and consider and perceived themselves as beneficiaries and petitioners, not as development participants or citizens. To tackle all the problems of the people in the rural areas, Governments both Central and State, develop plans centrally and not in a decentralised fashion. But it is an irony that some of our districts are larger than some countries in the world. Even within a state one finds a vast difference between or among the districts. Even within a district one finds much difference among the blocks. Genuine and effective decisions are taken, programmes are evolved, but to operationalise the same in different regions and sub-regions, concrete action plans are needed locally. Generic decisions, policies, programmes and schemes are chalked out but to dovetail them to the specific area, we need a specific action framework for implementation. Who will create such a plan at the district level and sub-district levels?

The 74th Amendment to the Constitution of India says that it is mandatory on the part of every District Planning Committee to prepare a development plan for the whole of the district. But there is no district plan machinery barring in a few states.

India has got a vast human resource but they are not being used profitably. In the era of globalization, for global products, markets are found even in remote villages. But to find a market for local products, there is no integrated system. As a result, cottage and village industries are ruined. Many traditional skills have disappeared. Village life is not self-reliant but is dependent. In this way villages have been transformed. In fact, villages have been deserted. All economic activities are city and town centric. Hence one finds large scale migration from villages to urban areas and urbanization becomes rapid by the day. Economic growth has picked up. But living conditions in the rural areas are becoming difficult. The majority in the villages are living in sub-human living conditions. These are the reasons for our stagnation in the Human Development Index.

Three centuries ago India and China retained half of the wealth and riches in the world with half of the population in the world[13]. Now India, though poised for 8 to 9 per cent growth, cannot proclaim that it has enabled the people to lead a decent and dignified human life. Yet 71 per cent of the population is living in the rural areas. Of them 58 per cent to 60 per cent rely on agriculture for their livelihood. Agriculture does not contribute substantially to economic growth and farmers have committed suicide due to crop failures due to the vagaries of the monsoon. The resulting large scale exodus of people to urban areas has made life in towns and cities miserable. The water level has gone down. Sanitation is poor in rural areas. Public schools have poor facilities and show ineffective functioning. Environmental degradation has set in. Skills in the rural areas have disappeared as they are not in demand. People have been reduced to beneficiaries and consumers rather than development participants. Still villages are in a feudal set-up as an agri-based economy is practiced and a hierarchical caste system plays a predominant role alongside patriarchy.

To bring about the needed change in the rural areas everyone looks to educational institutions. Why do we look to educational institutions for rural transformation despite the plethora of government programmes for rural development? For establishing effective linkage between the government and the communities we need catalyst institutions. The rural institutions can function as catalyst institutions. It does not mean that there are no higher educational institutions in the rural areas. There are many institutions in the rural areas but they are prototype Engineering Colleges, Arts and Science Colleges, Paramedical Training Institutions and even Medical Colleges. They are all just located in the rural areas. But there is absolutely no connection between the community and the educational institutions. Very near to the engineering colleges, villages are affected due to inadequate water supply and poor sanitation. This is not being attended to. It could be solved very easily by the intervention of the engineering colleges. Very near to medical colleges poor women and children are affected by anemia and malnutrition. They could be attended to by the medical colleges. In reality they are not doing so. These educational institutions are modelled on the colonial pattern, which always commanded the intellectual resources of the people and never sought to educate the natives and draw out the best from them. The system excludes Dalits, women and tribals. Further the structure of these educational institutions has not been democratized, but remain hierarchical, nurturing the feudal culture. They are not only feudal and exploitative but also patriarchal. The staff are career oriented. They do not connect themselves with the society in the absence of a mandate for outreach programmes. By overcoming all these problems, educational institutions have to be reorganized to meet the requirements of the community. It is to be recognized and understood that the educational institutions have a rich potential to be extended to the community. But, unfortunately, we do not have an institutional mechanism to transfer the rich potential or extendables in the form of ideas, technologies and skills to the rural communities. Before the introduction of new Rural Institutes, the existing educational institutions have to find a way to reach out to the communities.

In each and every college, a department can be created for outreach programmes as a special drive of the University Grants Commission, by which systematic steps can be taken to conduct outreach programmes in the communities very near to a college or university. By doing so many of the issues and problems can be investigated by the academic institutions and, based on the findings, policy advocacy can be done by the same institutions. By doing all these activities, universities and colleges can establish effective linkages with the society. Thus even the traditional and conventional colleges and universities can reach out to the society systematically through an institutional mechanism.

Then one can think about the establishment of Rural Institutes and Rural Universities.

Before planning the structure of the proposed new Rural Institutes, one has to analyse the functioning of the rural Institutions and the National Council for Rural Institutes. Before coming to evaluate the performance of the Rural Institutes one has to understand the reasons for many Rural Institutes merging with the traditional universities. The Rural Institutes were asked to work against the course of history. The direction of the Rural Institutes was quite opposite to the direction in which humanity moved.

The Rural Institutes were brought under the administrative system of the UGC, which is meant for conventional universities. The Rural Institutes which are in the ambit of the UGC have to move in the direction shown by the UGC. The leaders who are coming there for three years as Vice-Chancellors want to follow the guidelines of the UGC as it is the main funding agency instead of moving as per the objectives of the Rural Institutes. It is necessary that to manage the Rural Institutes, we identify persons with a deep understanding of the functioning of the Rural Institutes. But in reality, on many occasions, we cannot find persons with such a background to lead the Rural Institutes. Further the fundamental principles that shaped the edifice of the Rural Institute, the Gandhian framework, is yet another issue to be discussed. The whole Rural Institute concept is developed on the concept of "Nai Talim" of Gandhiji. The Rural Institutes came into being to cater to the needs of the students coming out from basic and post-basic education schemes. This amounted to developing a scheme of academic, research and extension activities on the principles of basic and post-basic education strongly rooted in 'Nai Talim' of Gandhiji. When basic and post-basic education were given a go-by how could Rural Institutes get students with such a background?

It is mandatory for the Rural Institutes to prepare the people for self-rule and build the capacity of the people to participate in the development process. But the development framework enunciated by Gandhiji has to be followed. The Rural Institutes have been brought under the framework of institutions which are in the process of modernization and industrialization. Having realized the weakness of this move, the National Council for Rural Institutes was created to set right the Rural Institutes. But the Rural Institutes were not brought under the domain of the NCRI. Thus NCRI became an entity like the

ICSSR, the ICHR and other institutions to provide funding support to the institutes working on the objectives and programmes of the funding agencies. Though the NCRI was initially under the guidance of Dr. Aram, former Vice-Chancellor of Gandhigram Rural University, and later of Mr. L.C. Jain, a noted Gandhian, the NCRI was not placed on a sound ideological and financial footing. Both of them were highly respected Gandhians and recognized persons in the policy making bodies. When they were in the NCRI they were close to the government also. They could have impressed upon the policy makers the need of strengthening of the NCRI and bringing the Rural Institutes under the ambit of the NCRI. Both of them struggled with the bureaucrats even for the normal functioning of the NCRI. As a result the NCRI emerged as a funding agency to sponsor some of the activities of the institutions which are well within the Gandhian framework of activities. That is why the officials are asking why we need the NCRI to fund educational institutions and NGOs as we have the UGC and the Rural Development Ministry to fund these institutions respectively. We could not create a set of institutions which are well within the framework of the NCRI.

The Central Government has declared that it would create world class management institutes, technology institutes, science institutes, central universities and so on. There is no mention about world class Rural Institutes to prepare cadres for rural development activities. Policy makers concentrate more on economic growth and human resource development in cities and towns and forget about the well-being of the people who are in the rural areas. Rural reconstruction and rural transformation need a totally different governance system, administrative system, livelihood system, economic system, credit system for which a new set of cadres are needed. An active interaction is needed between the academy and the communities. Gandhiji framed an ideal village system and this will be a referral point. This ideal village system has its own value framework. Keeping this in mind, the university has to work for it. One should not assume that the interaction between the institute and the community is free. There is the state, which takes up the responsibility of bringing development to the community. It takes decisions, evolves policies, prepares plans and allocates resources for all development activities. Yet development cannot be achieved. To achieve development, a catalyst action has to be performed by the Rural Institute. The New Panchayati Rai System has been established for which local body leaders and functionaries have to be trained and they are to be supported. As per the requirements of the Constitution of India, every district has to develop a development plan with the active participation of the people. For the preparation of the district plan, a planning machinery and a support structure are necessary. All development schemes require awareness among the people for implementation. The needed awareness has to be created. The available rural skills have to be enhanced. The skills have to be linked productively with the market system. A new support system is needed for farmers to come out from the present crises. A strong emphasis on research and development is required to support SHGs and village and cottage industries.

New Strategies and New Institutional Framework

To overcome the ill effects of climate change and global warming, micro actions are needed. The micro actions are to be carried out at the grassroots for which a support system is needed. To create a new cadre to manage the rural development activities, a strong academic programme is needed. It has to be totally contextual. To make use of the advantages of globalization, and to overcome the negative effects of globalization, steps have to be taken at the grassroots. It is not an easy job. Thus Rural Institutes have to take a new avatar to face the challenges. Otherwise they will be irrelevant and only to produce

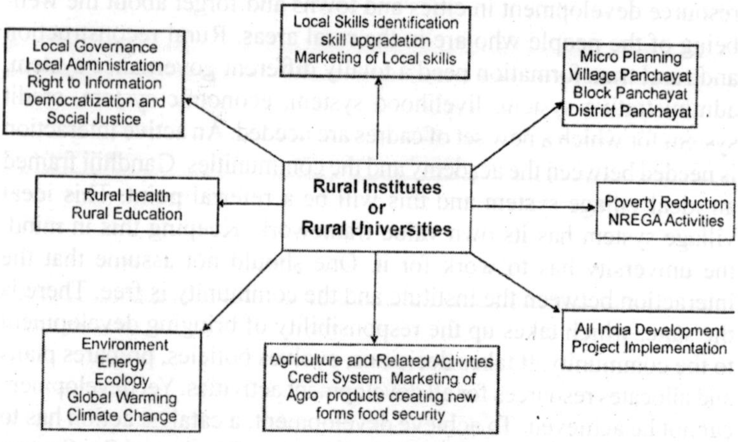

Diagram 9.1: A Blueprint for a New Rural University.

graduates as they are being produced in Arts and Science Colleges. So Rural Institutes should contextualize their programmes to face the challenges in the rural areas. They should be like the Indian Institute of Science, the Indian Institutes of Management, the Indian Institutes of Technology and so on. They need not ape the structure of traditional institutions. The structure should be simple and flexible. They should have a mechanism and strategy to assess the outcome or impact periodically. They should be dynamic and modern to tackle any issue that comes out of the rural communities. A blue print for the activities of a new Rural University is given hereunder.

By adopting the new strategies for outreach programmes the

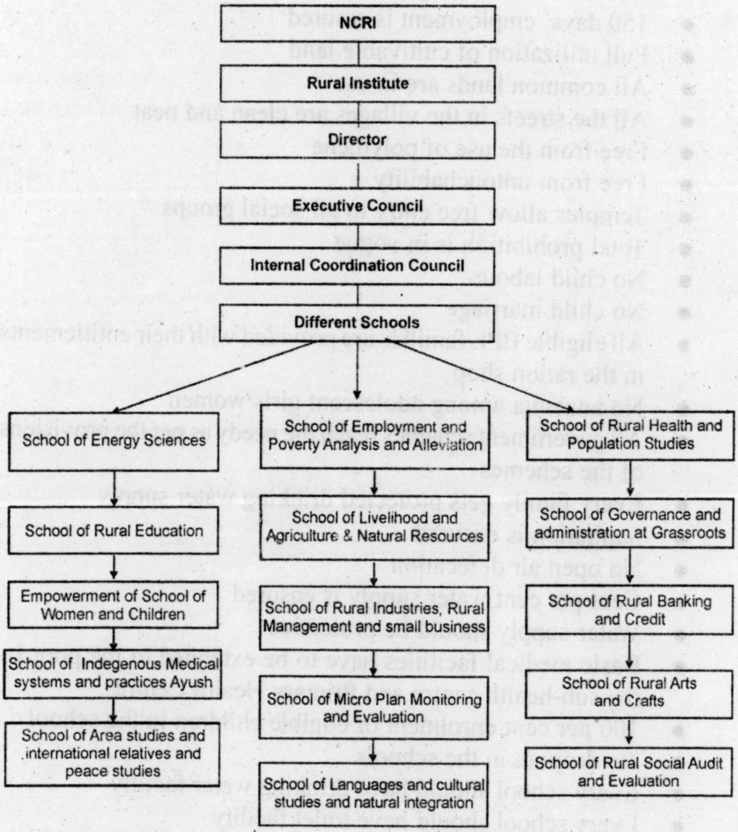

Diagram 9.2: Structure of Rural Institute.

traditional universities and colleges can perform extension activities to mitigate the socio-economic problems in the rural areas. In the same way, the new Rural Universities have to act through academic, research and outreach programmes with the aim of reducing the socio- economic problems of the rural communities. The institutions can work for better living conditions. By doing so ideal and model villages can be created. The indicators of an ideal or model village are given hereunder:

- No one suffers from hunger
- No one is affected by malnutrition
- No one is illiterate
- No one is affected by poverty
- 150 days' employment is assured
- Full utilization of cultivable land
- All common lands are in use
- All the streets in the villages are clean and neat
- Free from the use of polythene
- Free from untouchability
- Temples allow free entry to all social groups
- Total prohibition is in vogue
- No child labour
- No child marriage
- All eligible BPL families are provided with their entitlements in the ration shop
- No anaemia among adolescent girls/women
- All government schemes reach the needy as per the provisions of the schemes
- Every family gets protected drinking water supply
- Sanitation is ensured
- No open air defecation
- Cent per cent water supply is ensured
- Water supply should be protective
- Basic medical facilities have to be extended to the poor by the sub-health centre and Primary Health Centre
- 100 per cent enrolment of eligible children in the school
- No dropout in the schools
- Every school should have drinking water facility
- Every school should have toilet facility
- All villages tanks and ponds have to be desilted
- Youth club is every Gram Panchayat

- Women's club is every Gram Panchayat
- Artisans' guild is every Gram Panchayat
- Zero violence against women
- Zero violence against Dalits
- Gram Sabha meets regularly
- Gram Sabha ensures 50 per cent attendance
- Cent per cent voting in all elections
- No violence and no social conflict
- No registration of police case
- Recycling of water
- 100 per cent Institutional delivery
- Equal wages for men and women has to be ensured
- Zero female infanticide
- Information centre in every Gram Panchayat
- 100 per cent immunization Reducing Infant Mortality rate
- Reducing Maternal Mortality rate
- Reduce crude birth rate
- Improved sex ratio
- No HIV/AIDS affected person
- Well protected flora and fauna
- 100 per cent Antenatal care
- 100 per cent Postnatal care
- Every habitat in the villages has to have a connectivity pucca road
- Every habitat has to have electricity connection
- Every habitat should have telephone connection
- Every BPL family should have a ration card
- Every BPL family should have a health card
- Every BPL family should have a card of entitlements (Schemes meant for BPL families)
- Every Gram Panchayat area there should be a family counselling centre and counselling centre for women
- Every Gram Panchayat should have a perspective development plan document
- Every five year, there should be a development seminar in each Gram Panchayat to finalize a development plan
- In Gram Panchayat office every month income and expenditure has to be put up on the notice board

- All statutory committees of the Gram Panchayat have to perform their responsibilities. (Monitoring and supervising the implementation of government schemes and programmes and the functioning of the government institutions for the benefit of the rural masses)

All the above activities can be carried by the academic institutions in partnership with the Local Body Institutions. By doing so many of the MDG goals can be achieved easily.

Conclusion

Prior to the reshaping, reformulating and restructuring of the Rural Institutes, it is imperative to assess what is the need of the rural areas and communities and then one has to evaluate the opportunities in the form of policies, programmes, schemes and money allocations meant for rural development. The available resources in the educational institutions have to be assessed. The needs of the rural communities and the resources in the institutions have to be integrated for which appropriate devices and mechanisms have to be found. What has to be done by the Rural Institutes for effective implementation of the policies, programmes and schemes has to be identified and they are to be met. The resources may be in the form of ideas, skills, technology, services and so on. But the Rural Institute is distinct in contributing to regional development in all possible ways. Time and again it is repeated that regional development planning is the key activity for which the Rural Institutes have to help the local authority. Now it is all the more important since the Government of India has constitutionally created local bodies as self-governing institutions mandated with the preparation of district plans. Further the enactment of the NREGA has created another work of preparing projects for implementation. Every Gram Panchayat needs the help of the Rural Institutes. In order to achieve accountable governance and empower the people the Central Government enacted the Right to Information Act. To handle the RTI, people need awareness and support and that could also be provided by the Rural Institute. To combat the ill effects of climate change and global warming, local bodies have to work effectively and for that kind of activities Rural Institutes are all the more important. In this way academic programmes have to be designed, research programmes have to focus on the live issues of the rural communities and maintain constant interface with communities through outreach programmes. The Rural Institute concept is still under experiment. Having understood the potential of basic education and post-basic education based on 'Nai Talim', the experiment was started. But, till date, it did not attract the mainstream academy. As a result, it is still a subject for debate. Further, the 'Nai Talim' of Gandhiji has to be contextualized.

Rural Institutes should be created in India in the manner in which the Institutes of Management have been created. It should have the backing of an Act and preferably, an Act of Parliament. In each state there should be at least one Rural Institute. If need arises, in bigger states, two Rural Institutes can be created. But the Rural Institutes have to be evaluated in terms of their delivery and impact. The Rural Institutes have to help the traditional universities and colleges to conduct outreach programmes in a systematic way.

The Rural Institutes should be functionally and structurally reoriented and they are to be brought under the framework of the NCRI. The NCRI should be broad based and it should have the capacity to coordinate the activities of the Rural Institutes. It needs a thorough overhauling of the existing Rural Institutes and creating more number of Rural Institutes. These are to be coordinated functionally and financially. In this way Rural Institutes and National Council for Rural Institutes have to be reconstructed. A perfect monitoring and evaluation system has to be created. These Rural Universities have to be created through legislation and then only their stability and sustainability can be ensured.

Notes and References

1. K.N. Panikkar, "Towards a New Paradigm in Education", *The Hindu* (May 9, 2009). p. 12.
2. 'Nai Talim' is a scheme of educational programme designed by Mahatma Gandhi to prepare a self-reliant community by orienting body, mind and soul. Gandhiji wanted productive work and academic learning to be brought together into one integrated educational programme. When students begin to learn the three Rs, they should also begin productive work in appropriate fields. All educational programmes should be taught only in the mother tongue. M.K. Gandhi, *Village Swaraj*, Ahmedabad: Navajeevan Trust, 1962, pp. 74-91.

3. The Institute for Rural Management, Anand, and the Centre for Rural Management, Kottayam, are examples such of institutions which are not based on 'Nai Talim'.
4. Dr. S. Radhakrishnan's *University Education Commission* (1949), *Shrimali Committee* (1955), *Ramachandran's Committee* (1969) Reports.
5. It was mentioned in the *New Education Policy* (1986) and subsequently it was reiterated by the New Economic Policy's Programme of Action (PoA) in 1992.
6. In the Communication of Government of India, Ministry of Education, No. 55-5/47-3/3 dated 4th November, 1948, there was no mention of rural university, but in the section (IX) in the terms of reference, there was a mention of the need for more universities on a regional or other bases. Taking the cue from the above, a separate section was written.
7. Since Rural India had its own livelihood, culture, trade, skills, crafts and so on for 80 per cent of the population, the author of the chapter in the Radhakrishnan Commission wanted to bring about transformation and reconstruction keeping the core values of India in focus and for this he suggested a new framework of education for rural development. Further the whole edifice of the framework has to be anchored on the concept of 'Nai Talim'. As per this chapter, the expansion of higher education should have been on this framework. But, unfortunately, it did not take place. Later there were different versions of the need for Rural Universities. One set of arguments is that it has to educate the rural masses formally and informally. Another set of arguments is that this university has to have live linkages with communities. It has to conduct outreach programmes. Yet another argument is projected about the role of rural university: it has to extend ideas, information, technology, skill, capacity and so on, to the rural communities through its outreach programmes and students learn by doing such activities. There is one more argument that it has to do research on rural development issues and help the community and the government to achieve the target of their activities.
8. Arun Kumar Dave, "A Rural University—Need of the Nation" *Ailaan* Vol. II: No. 11 (February, 2009).
9. National Council of Rural Institute, *A New Dawn on Rural Higher Education from Chaos to Order,* Hyderabad: National Council of Rural Institutes, 2001.
10. P.V. Narasimha Rao, "*Rural Universities: My Vision*". Inaugural Address. Hyderabad: National Council of Rural Institutes, 1995.
11. Ram Takwale, "Nai Talim of Connected Society with Education for Transformation", *Ailaan* Vol. II: No. 1 (January 2009).

12. With the support of the Ford Foundation, serious studies have been conducted on the implications of globalisation and as a result a newsletter is being circulated among the Panchayats entitled '*Global and Local*'.
13. World Bank, *Reshaping Economic Geography: World Development Report,* 2009. Washington, DC: The World Bank, 2009.

10

Extension in Higher Education: The Missing Dimension

People in India and those at the grassroots in particular, are living in a paradoxical situation. Opportunities for amassing wealth and possibilities of marginalizing or excluding people from the process of development are brighter as the new economic movement of liberalization, privatization and globalization, is fast catching up. Those who understand the process easily exploit the opportunities and amass wealth whereas those who do not understand the process and lack the capacity are totally marginalized and excluded from the process of development. The developed societies, with their economic advancement, speedy technological development, perfect handling of the technology and enhanced capacity have outwitted the developing societies in terms of development. The gap between the technology and the capacity of the people to handle the technology is wider in developing societies.

The growing population and the unsound and unscientific development policies for speedy growth in the developing countries have caused great damage to the ecology and the environment. Further, in the name of development, natural resources have been exploited to the maximum. People in the rural areas are mostly unskilled and they rely on agriculture for their livelihood. The semi-skilled people and the skilled ones are not in a position to make use of their skills as they are outdated. All public institutions have failed the people as private schools private industries, and private hospitals are flourishing. Institutions which were created for delivery of public services have failed miserably. People prefer to rely on the private sector for everything on payment. Yet the public institutions are eating away the public exchequer. People's capability and opportunity to earn their livelihood is grim but will be forced to pay even to get minimum of essential services for meeting their basic needs. The use of plastics and polythene bags has created a menace to the environment. The total livelihood system of the poor has been damaged. The communities in the rural areas and the slums in the urban areas are facing scores of problems. Most of the problems are related to lack of awareness and poor skills among the people. Many of the problems of the communities and especially the poor can be solved very easily if the educational institutions are involved in community service through systematic extension activities. Medical colleges, through their extension activities, could treat poor patients at their place through their transportation. Agricultural colleges can disseminate technical know-how to the farming communities through their scientists. Arts and science colleges can create awareness among the people regarding their livelihood. Technical institutions can develop appropriate technologies and hand them over to the rural people. Moreover, they can equip the people with greater skills with self-employment potentials. Total literacy can be achieved with the active participation of higher education institutions. In many of the southern states, this could be achieved within a short span of time. Awareness about the decent living conditions of the human beings can be created among the people.

Even after fifty four years of democratic governance and implementation of series of rural development schemes for the poor, still people live in sub-human living conditions. On the contrary, the number of educational institutions are on the rise. Engineering colleges, medical colleges, para professional colleges, private universities and other higher educational institutions have been constantly growing. At present, many of the institutions have been started in the rural areas as they get adequate water free of cost and space. When more and more educational institutions are in the process of producing graduates, the society gets more literacy and qualified personnel for service. But why then the problems of the poor are also growing and becoming so critical? There are a number of factors responsible for the conditions of the poor in the society, of which, the non-existence of the linkage between the society and the educational institutions will be one of the prime factors.

All the higher educational institutions have several extendable aspects, namely information, knowledge, skills, technology, service and so on. But the institutional structure is not oriented to extend the best to the society. Further, the institutions do not have the mechanism to convert the available extendables in a form suitable to the requirements of the community. Many believe that the Agriculture Faculty alone can do extension work. Every department and discipline can do extension work provided they know the strategy and the method. Even in the UGC framework, extension is assigned only to the Adult and Continuing Education Department. Unfortunately, in many State Universities, this department has been closed.

Thus extension, the third and vital dimension of higher education, is neglected now. The gap between the higher education institutions

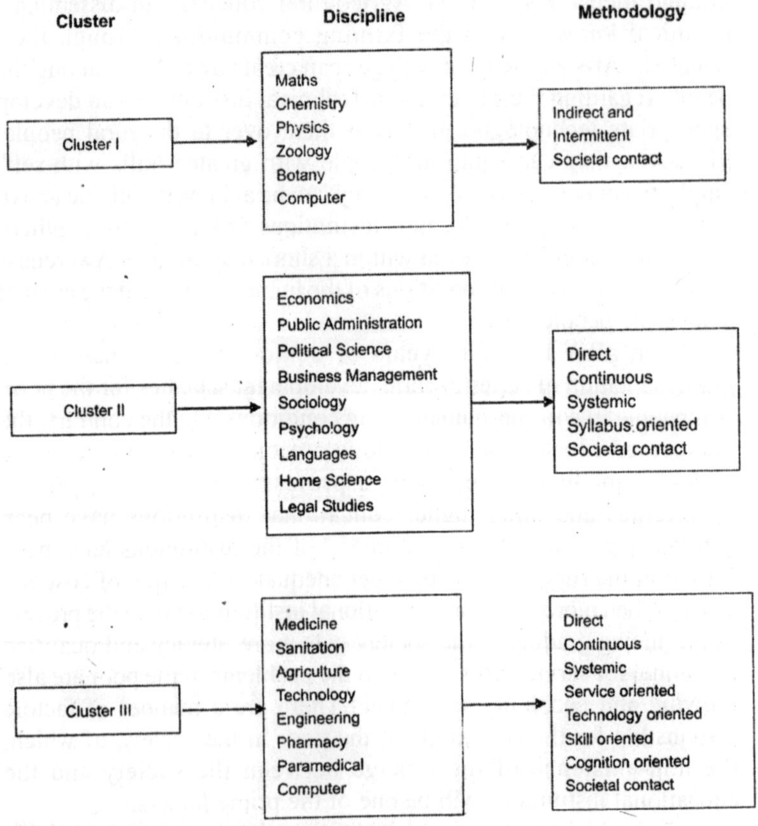

Diagram 10.1: Classification of Clusters

and the society, therefore, has to be bridged. The extendables available in the higher education institutions have to be extended to the society for the benefit of both through a system of Extension Education and Extension Service. In order to perform the above tasks, the disciplines in the higher education have to be reclassified. Higher educational institutions can be grouped according to their nature and character. Some of the institutions can create awareness among the people. Many of the institutions and departments can deliver services directly to the people. A few institutions and departments can transfer skills and build the capacity of the rustic folk who perform difficult roles and tasks.

Table 10.1: Strategies

I	Continuously working with a target group	Institutions and departments continuously working with the target group, namely, ultra-poor, women, dalits, children, disabled, artisans and farmers
II	Continuously working on an issue	Institutions and departments can work on issues, namely, sanitation, water supply, poverty reduction, agriculture, skills upgradation, education, etc.
III	Delivering services on wheels	Institutions and departments can place the extension materials in their vehicles, visit communities and offer their services and at their doorsteps
IV	Dissemination of information	Institutions and departments can provide useful, processed and packaged information to the different stakeholders in society
V	Building the skills and capacity	Institutions and departments can build the skills and capacity of stakeholders and service providers and user groups
VI	Skills upgradation	Institutions and departments can reinvent old skills, reinvigorate skills and upgrade the skills which are in vogue to the level of the market conditions
VII	Assisting the delivery system	Institutions and departments can provide assistance to service providers, in the form of technology, skills and capacity
VIII	Assisting development organizations	Institutions and departments can assist the development organizations and institutions which are working in the rural areas by building their skills and capacity
IX	Establishing forward and backward linkages	Institutions and departments can create and promote linkages among the institutions and organizations working for the poor

Table 10.2: Gist: Information, Awareness, Skill, Capacity, Technology and Service

Sl. No.	*Activities*	*Institutions/Departments*
1.	Farm Input Farm Activities Farm Practices Farm Technology	Agriculture Faculty
2.	Animal Husbandry	Veterinary Faculty/College/University
3.	Water supply and Sanitation Water recycling Waste disposal	Civil Department in Engineering College Sanitation Department in Medical College Medical College Chemistry Department in Arts and Science College
4.	Ante natal care Natal care Post natal care	Medical College Home Science Department Centre for Women Studies
5.	Child Care	Medical College Home Science Department
6.	Youth Development	Department of Youth Affairs/Development
7.	Panchayat Management Governance	Public Administration Political Science
7A.	Adult Literacy	Adult and Continuing Education
7B.	Rights of Women, Children and Dalits	Legal Studies
8.	Women Empowerment SHG activities Management Gender equality	Women Studies Centres Home Science Department Sociology Department
9.	Natural Resources Management	Environmental Studies Centres Botany Department
10.	Public Distribution System Poverty surveys Poverty reduction strategies	Economics Department
11.	Use of solar energy Energy Management Energy Technology	Physics Department Energy Department
12.	Peoples' skills and technology for Economic Activities	Rural Industries and Management Department
13.	Herbal alternative medicine Nature cure	Pharmacy Department Botany Department Zoology Department

Sl. No.	*Activities*	*Institutions/Departments*
14.	Best practices in the community for livelihood Tribal studies and welfare Conflict resolution	Sociology Department Anthropology Department Gandhian Studies/Peace Studies Department
15.	Imbibing cooperative spirit and inculcating repayment ethics among borrowers	Cooperation Department
16.	Taking information, communication, technology (ICT) to rural areas	Computer Centres
17.	Micro level planning Resource surveys	Rural Development Department Geography Department
18.	Population awareness Family welfare promotion	Demography Department
19.	Prevention and promotion of Culture and Art Awareness about national leaders, freedom fighters	History Department

The above list is only an illustrative but not exhaustive.

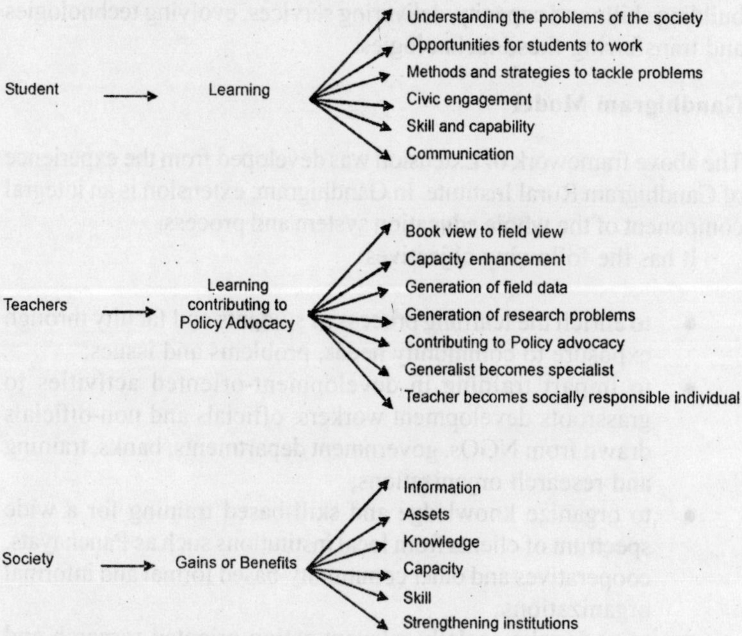

Diagram 10.2: Benefits Win-Win

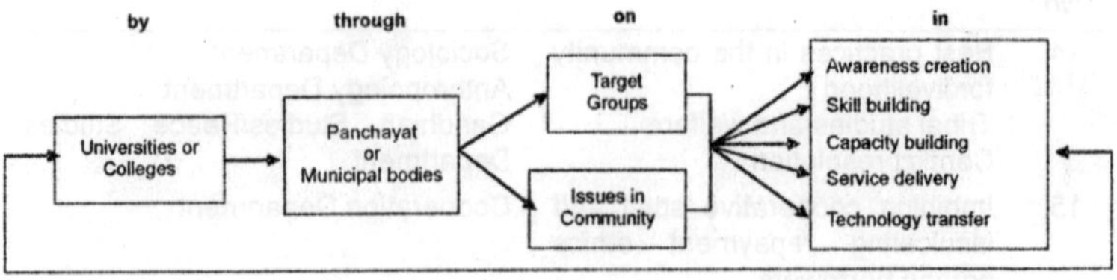

Fig. 10.3: A Framework for Extension

A Framework for Extension

Higher Educational Institutions used to have a linkage with the grassroots institutions both in the rural and urban areas for their extension activities on a sustainable basis. Every institution should have a clear cut approach for its extension activities. While carrying out extension activities, the higher educational institutions can either work in a social group or in a geographical area on issues facing the community. Their activities may encompasses creating awareness, building skills and capacity, delivering services, evolving technologies and transferring these technologies.

Gandhigram Model

The above framework of Extension was developed from the experience of Gandhigram Rural Institute. In Gandhigram, extension is an integral component of the whole education system and process.

It has the following objectives:

- to enrich the learning process of students and faculty through exposure to community needs, problems and issues;
- to impart training in development-oriented activities to grassroots development workers, officials and non-officials drawn from NGOs, government departments, banks, training and research organizations;
- to organize knowledge and skill-based training for a wide spectrum of clients from local institutions such as Panchayats, cooperatives and other community-based formal and informal organizations;
- to undertake socially relevant action-oriented research and analysis for the betterment of the rural community; and

- to bring out changes in the living conditions of different sections of the rural community.

Methods

The above objectives are being realized through a series of activities by adopting the following methods:

1. Women Melas (of SHGs)
2. Field visits
3. Camps
4. Awareness camps
5. Training programmes
6. Rallies and processions
7. Skill building workshops
8. Capacity building workshops

Target Groups of Training Programmes

Training programmes are organized for the following personnel:

- Farmers and landless labourers
- Rural artisans
- Rural women and children
- Student and non-student youth
- Leaders and representatives of grassroots organizations
- Presidents, Ward Members and other non-officials of the Panchayat system at different levels
- Officials at different levels of administration of various rural development departments of the government
- Technocrats and officials of water supply and sanitation departments
- NGO functionaries
- Extension functionaries
- Researchers
- Teachers of colleges and universities.

Type of Skills Imparted

Training programmes are organized on the following skills:

- Bakery
- Hand-made paper
- Soap making
- Oil extraction
- Herbal products
- Tailoring
- Toy making
- Fruit preservation
- Food processing
- Glass blowing
- Pottery
- Blacksmithy
- Carpentry
- Repair of cycles
- Repair and maintenance of scientific and electronic gadgets
- Repair/service of TV, radio and emergency lamps, etc.

Spectrum of Strategies

Prominent among the strategies disseminated are:

- Sustainable agriculture
- Promotion of agricultural productivity through organic farming
- Indigenous technical knowledge in agriculture
- Post harvest technology
- Mushroom cultivation
- Watershed management
- Wasteland development
- Rain water harvesting
- Waste water recycling
- Vermicomposting
- Skill upgradation of rural artisans
- Income generation programmes
- Environmental sanitation
- Environmental pollution and water quality monitoring
- Pollution control measures
- Fluoride toxicity prevention and control
- Rural water supply and sanitation
- Reproductive and child health

- Population education
- Nutrition
- Rural leadership
- Panchayati Raj
- Multi-level planning
- Participatory micro plan
- Participatory Rural Appraisal
- Micro credit management
- Micro enterprises
- Rural entrepreneurship
- Community based organizations
- Computer literacy to rural women and rural school children
- Computer training for employment generation in rural areas
- Cost effective technology
- Non-conventional energy.

Table 10.3: Illustrative List of Activities done by the Department at Gandhigram Rural Institute

1.	Department of Political Science	Building the capacity of Local Body Leaders and helping the Gram Panchayats to prepare perspective plan
2.	Department of Rural Industries and Management	Training village youth and SHG women in skills to develop micro enterprises and village industries.
3.	Department of Extension Education monitoring and evaluation of projects	Training the NGO representatives in management of rural projects, preparation of rural development projects for NGOs, donor agencies and government and monitoring and evaluation of projects.
4.	Department of Agriculture and Animal Husbandry	To train farmers to increase productivity and to sustain profit and to train SHG women in dairying.
5.	Department of Sanitation	Developing low cost sanitary material and conducting training to local body leaders and engineers of Government Departments.
6.	Department of Sociology	Creating awareness among the marginalized about their rights and opportunities for development.
7.	Department of Cooperation	Training the functionaries in cooperatives, creating awareness on repayment ethics.

(*Contd.*)

Table 10.3: (*Contd.*)

8.	Rural Technology Centre	Developing cost effective technology and propagating in village communities.
9.	Department of Home Science	Creating awareness among the women about their results and opportunities.
10.	Department of Biology	Training the SHG women in Horticulture, Vermiculture, Sericulture and Biotechnology.
11.	Department of Physics	Installing smokeless chulahs and training village women in using the same.
12.	Department of Chemistry	Creating awareness among the people about environment and helping the local community to get safe drinking water supply.
13.	Department of Mathematics	Training school teachers in villages in Mathematics teaching and about latest development.
14.	Department of Computer Science	Training the rural youth and SHG women in computer operations.
15.	Department of Economics	Identification of vulnerable families.
16.	Department of Rural Development	Helping the Panchayats in micro level plan and women empowerment.
17.	Department of Applied Research	Taking up social problems for action research.
18.	Department of Gandhian Thought and Peace Science	Taking Gandhiji's ideals to villages and working for conflict resolution.

Resource Mobilization

Enormous amounts of resources are available at every level for public service. In the era of globalization, resource mobilization is not a difficult task. The Government provides enormous amounts of money for IEC activities that can be tapped. All companies have to spend a portion of their profit for social service as a mandate and they are ready to provide resources. The banking sector has a specific allocation for such service activities to the society. There are non-governmental organizations and voluntary organizations which can be used for this purpose. There are a lot of funding agencies in the country to support extension activities which can be tapped efficiently. Lion's Clubs and Rotary Clubs can also be used. For many of the activities, people themselves will contribute. At the university level and the college level what is needed is commitment and a sense of dedication with a set of strategies. Gandhigram has been supported by a slew of donors both governmental and non-governmental in the promotion of scores of activities listed above (Their list is annexed for the benefit of those interested in contacting up them for their proposed activities).

Outcome of this Extension

Extension services in rural communities will generate an array of benefits to the people in difficulties. Villages will get clean drinking water supply. 100 per cent literacy will be achieved. All eligible children will be enrolled in schools. There won't be any malnourished children in the rural areas and any anaemic patient among pregnant women. IMR will be reduced and babies will be born in the rural areas with correct weight. Shelter can be provided to all. PDS shops will provide the entitlements to the poor. The skills of the people will be used profitably. They will gain access to the market will be provided with the needed technology for their secured livelihood and they will start living in humane conditions. People will have development aspirations and they will be conscious of development. The marginalized, poor, women and dalits will be empowered. People will have necessary awareness on their rights and duties. Students and teachers will know the social reality in all its aspects and they will be conscious of social service. A responsible good society and good governance can be established by ensuring the university system to be more responsive to the needs and problems of the community and the interests and demands of the society.

Conclusion

Thus every college and every university has to first assess what they can extend to the society and identify the extendables, namely ideas, knowledge, information, skill, capacity, technology and strategy. Further the institutions have to evolve appropriate methodological designs to do extension activities. It is further necessary to identify the partner institutions and organizations to carry out the extension activities by providing necessary resources and wherewithals. Finally, the extension activities have to be integrated with the curriculum for its sustainability. So that most of the ills facing the society could be easily solved.

Annexure-1

Gandhigram Partners

For all the above activities the following agencies have helped:

- Central Social Welfare Board, New Delhi
- Coconut Development Board, Cochin
- Cooperative Development Foundation, Hyderabad
- Council for Advancement of Peoples Action and Rural Technology (CAPART), New Delhi and Hyderabad
- Danish International Development Agency (DANIDA), Tirunelveli and Cuddalore
- Department of Forestry, Kerala
- Department of Rural Development, Tamil Nadu
- Department of Science and Technology, New Delhi
- District Rural Development Agencies
- Ford Foundation, New Delhi
- Gandhigram Trust, Gandhigram
- Housing and Urban Development Corporation, New Delhi
- The Hunger Project, New Delhi
- Indian Council for Agricultural Research, New Delhi
- Indian Council for Social Sciences Research, New Delhi
- Khadi and Village Industries Commission, Mumbai
- M.S. Swaminathan Research Foundation, Chennai
- Ministry of Rural Areas and Employment, New Delhi
- Ministry of Social Welfare, New Delhi
- Ministry of Youth Affairs and Sports, New Delhi
- National Bank for Agriculture and Rural Development, Mumbai
- National Commission for Women, New Delhi
- National Council for Rural Institutes, Hyderabad
- National Wasteland Development Board, New Delhi
- NGOs in Tamil Nadu and other States
- Planning Commission, India, New Delhi
- Population Foundation of India, Mumbai
- Rajiv Gandhi National Drinking Water Mission, New Delhi
- State Social Welfare Board, Chennai
- Tamil Nadu Integrated Nutrition Project, Chennai
- Tamil Nadu Adi-Dravidar Housing Development Corporation, Chennai
- Tamil Nadu Corporation for Women Development, Chennai
- Tamil Nadu Council for Science and Technology, Chennai
- Tamil Nadu Water and Drainage Board, Chennai
- TTK Hospital, Chennai
- United Nations International Children's Emergency Fund, Chennai and New Delhi
- United Nations Fund for Population Activities (UNFPA)
- University Grants Commission, New Delhi
- World Bank, New Delhi

11

Reinventing and Contextualizing the Rural Universities

Introduction

'Rural Institute' and 'Rural University' had been in discourse and operation along with the mainstream higher education system for the past sixty years in India. Though ideally the concepts had been spoken, the Rural Institute system had not been widely recognized strengthened as a system of higher education and yet many such institutes were created at the dawn of independence. Over a period of time the newly created institutes had moved over to the mainstream system of higher education and a few are in operation which do not reflect the spirit of the Rural Institute and they exist in form and not in spirit as they are being supported financially by the Central Government. In order to activate the Rural Institutes another attempt was made by creating National Council for Rural Institutes (NCRI) yet the conditions have not been improved. It is high time to make a realistic evaluation as to what extent the Rural Institutes are useful to the society for rural reconstruction and rural from formation. If it is useful why the Rural Institutes have not been strengthened? What are the problems faced by the existing institutions? How are these institutions performing and how they are placed in the higher education system in India at present are to be analysed in this article.

Historical Background

Still confusion remains on the concept 'Rural Institute.' Being an academic working in a Rural Institute for about 20 years I could make out the nature of confusion from the level of the head of the institution to the last person working in the institute. Only a few academics understand and they too are not able to operationalise the concept into reality in their domain of activities. Some argue that Rural Institute is meant for achieving rural development and many perceive that it is meant for rural poor boys and girls. A few argue that it is nothing but preparing manpower for rural development. Yet Gandhians argue that it is the development of the post basic education conceptualized based on the Gandhian Frameworks of Education. It is a new kind of exercise to evolve alternative model of education. Rural Institutes have to prepare manpower for achieving rural transformation through Gandhian perspective. Thus fourteen Rural Institutes (ten plus four) had been started in India at the dawn of Independence. These fourteen Rural Institutes supposed to be the alternative system of education in India based on the Gandhian Framework of Education. Unfortunatively, of the fourteen, one institute remained as rural higher education institute and all other institutions had transformed themselves to join with the mainstream system of education in India. The remaining one is also functioning neither as a Rural Institute nor as a full-fledged university. It tries to ape the traditional universities but it tries to keep certain values of the Rural Institute developed over a period of time. Now almost Rural Institute as a distinct category of educational institution based on the framework evolved for Rural Institutes in India is an extinct entity. But there are many institutions carrying the label but do not reflect the characteristics. They are both in the government fold and in the domain of Non-Governmental Organizations. At present many do not know what is Rural University or Rural Institute and what for it was created? To get clarity one has to trace from authentic source. In my opinion we have to trace the concept and explanation from the writings and speeches of the founders of the Rural Institute.

No doubt (Rural University System) is not a system adopted or adapted from any other system outside India. It is indigenous in origin. It is in Indian tradition of educational system. India has its own rich knowledge tradition. No civilization can flourish without a knowledge base. Wide references are available for Gurukula system, the great hermitage of scholars and philosophers functioning in India. In the same way world renowned universities like those of Nalanda and Taxila functioned in Indian region. These institutions drew scholars from all over the world. The Rural University system which we talk about was in the blood and bone of the history of India. Our culture and civilization rooted in the rural life of the people. All our activities were around the villages. It was only during the British the rural areas were more and more neglected and attention was paid only to a few hundred towns and cities. Since a few development activities were initiated in the urban areas, people in the rural areas started migrating to urban centres. When higher education institutions were created in a few towns and cities, people who know the implications of higher education moved out of the rural areas only with a specific purpose of educating their children in the urban centres. As a result rural masses were totally neglected and kept far away from the reach of higher education.

Though millions of the people were having aspiration to enjoy higher education they were compelled to remain in the rural areas as their livelihood depended on agriculture. They were not able to migrate from the rural areas. In order to cater to the needs of the rural masses, an education system was needed that too in the rural area itself and that too without affecting their livelihood and their rural activities. Nowhere it was in the thought process of the leaders and opinion markers. It was only a few Gandhian workers based on the system evolved by M.K. Gandhi reacted to the mainstream system of education imported, introduced and practiced in India by the British and subsequently it was followed by our Political paundits.

There were bold initiatives like Gurukula University at Haridwar created by Arya Samajists, the Visva-Bharati University at Santiniketan established by the great poet and philosopher Rabindranath Tagore, the National University at Adayar established by Dr. Annie Beasant. There was yet another path breaking event, namely establishing Vidya Peeths of Gujarat and Bihar and subsequently Jamia Millia of Dr. Zakir Hussain. Attempts were there in history to provide an alternative system of education to the British system of education in India.[1]

'Rural University' or 'Rural Institute' was fundamentally a concept (to be debated) which gained currency among the policy makers and Gandhian academics for some time in India after the submission of the report of the University Education Commission under the chairmanship of Dr. Sarvapalli Radhakrishnan.[2] The Dr. Radhakrishnan Committee Report is one of the acclaimed reports in India in terms of its vision. In this report a chapter on 'Rural

University' was incorporated. It was written by one of the commission members Dr. Arthor E. Morgan, the President of the Tennessee River Valley Authority in the USA. He visualized an ideal university suited to Indian ethos. It is yet another paradox that a foreigner was able to show us the way. In this chapter an argument was advanced that the existing universities, focused on cities and towns and not on villages and the whole educational system was devised to prepare personnel for Government jobs and not for social transformation. Morgan urged that India needed a different, distinct, independent institution to prepare cadre of leaders to bring about transformation in the Indian Rural Society.[3] For three years from the advent of independence it was only a concept in the making till Nanabhai Bhatt translated the idea of the Rural Institute into action in 1951 in Gujarat. In his preface to the booklet entitled "Gram Vidhyapith" he dwelt upon the foundation of the Rural University. According to him, the edifice of the Rural University should be built on 'Nai Talim', the basic principle enunciated by Gandhiji. Bhatt unequivocally stated that the existing university culture had not shaped the younger generation with character, humility, commitment, responsibility and spirituality which was necessary to reconstruct the Indian society. It was to be recognized that the dreams of the founding fathers would be realized not through a few government servants and a few development schemes of the government, but only by invoking and involving the masses, for which a cadre of leaders and volunteers with a sense of commitment and values was needed.

Morgan's chapter on Rural Institutes has eight sections. In the first section he explains the context in which 'Rural Institutes' are visualised. The conditions of the villages and the basic education programme are explained. Undoubtedly it is all based on the Gandhian framework of rural reconstruction. India being a primarily rural society, has to be reconstructed in such a manner that the development achieved should be sustainable. The whole vision was against the on-going development process of modernization, industrialization, and Westernization. It was to be almost a turning point in history.

In the second section post-basic education is explained. The third section deals with rural industrialization. The fourth division explains the reconstruction of Indian villages. The fifth section is the core area which deals with the establishment of Rural Colleges and Universities. In this section the characteristics, the curriculum and the methodology are explained. The sixth section deals with the basic concerns of Rural Universities. What kind of management and administrative systems have to be developed to manage the rural educational institutions, is explained. The final section wraps up the whole argument. The whole chapter challenges Gandhian educationists to conceptualize new education programmes which are to be integrated with the entire education system and policies of the government. It is to be noted here that the mainstream education followed the model of the West. The British system of education had been adopted and was in vogue. For the new education system every aspect had to be worked out and integrated with the existing system so that it could be acceptable to policy makers for evolving policies and allocating resources for strengthening the new educational system. As per this chapter, if the new framework for establishment of Rural Higher Education Institutions raised hopes among policy makers, the entire education system would be totally oriented towards the Gandhian framework. Unfortunately the Gandhian educationists did not concretize the new education system and hence the western model picked up vigour as it was well within the existing framework of the development process of the world.

In 1954 the Government of India appointed a committee under the chairmanship of Dr. K.L. Shrimali to look into higher rural education and offer recommendations. The Committee submitted its report and suggested an umbrella institutional set up to coordinate the Rural Institutes' academic activities. Based on the recommendation of the Shrimali Committee the National Council for Rural Higher Education (NCRHE) was established in 1955. In the first phase the National Council for Rural Higher Education identified ten institutions called "Rural Institutes" which would be later developed into rural universities. The ten institutions were:

1. Shri Niketan (West Bengal)
2. Jamia Millia Islamia (New Delhi)
3. Mouni Vidyapith (Gargoti, Kolhapur)
4. Shivaji Lok Vidyapith (Amravati)
5. Gandhigram (Madurai)
6. Vidyabhawan (Udaipur)
7. Ramakrishna Mission Vidyalaya (Coimbatore)
8. Lok Bharti (Sanosara, Saurashtra)
9. Toorki (Bihar)

10. Balwani Vidyapith (Bichpuri, Agra)

Within a short span of time the Rural Institutes faced a plethora of problems because they were not in the broader framework of the Indian Education System. In 1958, the problems of the Rural Institutes were discussed in an International Seminar at Bichpuri. The Rural Institutes could not move further in the existing framework as they were caught in the bureaucratic net and, as a result, the Rural Institutes faced innumerable hurdles. Having experienced turbulent weather, the Rural Institutes had decided to be merged with the traditional university system within fifteen years of their existence without creating much impact and they turned towards the Western mode of educational system by changing into constituent colleges of affiliated universities[4].

If an analysis is made as to why the Rural Institutes could not survive, one would meet with surprises. It is necessary to keep the basic objectives as referral points for evaluation. The objective was to create a cadre of Rural Development leaders and managers to tackle the problems of the rural communities. Programmes were to be offered not to seek employment opportunity in Government Departments. They would be real change makers to bring about rural transformation. But the main reason attributed for the failure was that the graduates who passed out of the Rural Institutes were not able to get admission to the traditional university system in Government Departments. From these arguments one can infer easily that the students admitted to the Rural Institutes were not moulded, motivated, oriented and trained towards the objectives of the Rural Institutes. The students who got admitted to the Rural Institutes were also having the same objective of seeking jobs in the government system as the students in the traditional educational institutions.

The Gandhigram Rural Institute was the only institute that continued as a Rural Institute and delivered what it ought to deliver to the rural masses at a limited level with the dedicated staff under the leadership of Dr. G. Ramachandran. The staff who worked in the Rural Institute could not get remuneration as their counterparts elsewhere and yet they served the institute with a sense of commitment. Despite all trials and tribulations it tried its best to retain the characteristics of the Rural Institute. At that point of time it was well appreciated. Hence the University Grants Commission granted it the status of a Deemed

University. Even at that point, a distinct structure could have been created suitable to the Rural Institutes' objectives. Instead the Gandhigram Rural Institute opted to follow the model of the conventional universities. This prompted the Gandhigram Rural Institute to make a slow departure from the basic characteristics of the Rural Institute.

The courses offered in the beginning were changed by citing the reasons stated by earlier Rural Institutes and, gradually, barring a few, all the degrees up to the masters came to be modelled on those of the traditional universities. The appointment of the Vice-Chancellor has played a crucial role in deciding the fate of the Rural Institutes. On many occasions Vice-Chancellors were appointed without any Rural Institute background. They managed the institute to suit their own philosophy. As a result the institutions were caught in the dilemma of either to go back to a 'Rural Institute' character or transform into a conventional university which they really could not do. One has to understand the challenges for the Rural Institutes had to be faced by the leaders of the Institutes by their innovative and committed action. They needed the support of the Government. In this context it is necessary to recognize and assess the honest attempts made by different institutions.

Assessment of the First Phase

Rural Higher Education gained momentum in Gujarat by the setting up of Gram Vidyapiths. Lok Bharti, though it remained an inspiring concept, could not leap forward despite the attempts made continuously. Three Gram Vidyapiths were established in Gujarat. They were in Bahadurpur (Baroda District), Samoda (Mehsana District) and Vedchi (Surat District). A Gram Vidyapith Society was formed to strengthen the initiatives of these Vidyapiths. To further their activities the Gujarat State Basic Education Board was sought to be established to coordinate the activities of 'Nai Talim' right from primary to Rural Higher Education. The proposal for establishing the Board statutorily failed miserably. The Rural Institutes created with enthusiasm, commitment and sincerity were not projected with a positive message to the policy makers and the people that the new scheme of education would deliver the goods and solve the problems of the rural communities.

The students who passed out of these institutions faced many problems as they were from a totally different stream from the mainstream framework of Higher Education in India. Many students from the Rural Institutes who wanted to pursue higher studies found it difficult to get admission to the conventional universities. Many who tried to get government jobs by showing the degree obtained from Rural Institutes could not get them. This has been projected as a reason for the drifting away from the concept of the 'Rural Institute'. This has been projected as the failure of the Rural Institutes. The real issue, however, is that the Rural Institutes had not performed as they ought to. In the name of Rural Institutes they performed the job of a college affiliated to a conventional university. It is also a paradox that these Rural Institutes which were expected to perform the unique role of Rural Institutes were brought under the rubric of the UGC. The UGC pattern is different and totally opposite to the direction of the Rural Institutes. In order to get funds, the Rural Institutes had to adhere to the norms of the UGC and, as a result, the Rural Institute experiments were diluted. As a result, they could not register any visible impact. They could not improve sanitation or livelihood, protect rural industries, innovate appropriate technology, provide health facilities, literacy, and work for social change. They existed as show pieces. Beyond a certain time they merged with the conventional institutions. The old institutions like the Gandhigram Rural Institute and the new ones like the Chitrakoot Institute struggled to survive as they did not have appropriate leadership excepting the Vice-Chancellors. They too were mere managers for three years to run the show. They could not improve the functioning substantially. They could not provide ideological leadership for the Rural Institute. But due to the liberal funding of the UGC, they improved the infrastructure and enabled the staff to improve their career. They could not come out with academic programmes which could foster skills needed for reconstructing the rural areas and transforming the rural landscape. Sometimes, to justify their distinctiveness, the Rural Institutes introduced courses and programmes with a rural bias but the students could not get gainful employment. Ultimately, the students, coming to the Rural Institutes were from the lowest level of performance in schools with very little motivation.

Rural Institutes are being viewed as non-profitable white elephants. Only students with a low academic profile and low motivation join the institutes. Further, the rural institutes are driven by the funding agencies to produce more number of students as do the colleges. This kind of drive completely pushes the Rural Institutes away from the traditional institutions of learning. Hence affiliating these Rural Institutes to the traditional university system was inevitable and imperative from the perspective of the students' future as they did not have the needed motivation and commitment to serve in the rural areas for rural reconstruction and transformation. Here one has to recognize and underline that Rural Institutes were created not to train students to get clerical positions in government offices. They were to become change agents in the rural areas. But, unfortunately, a perception was developed that the students who got degrees and diplomas have to go for higher studies or get employment opportunity in the government sector. When Rural Institutes were seen from that perspective, many felt that the students faced problems. Moreover, many wanted to move with the mainstream education rather than carve out a different path distinctively different from the mainstream educational system. Even the degrees and diplomas in Rural Institutes were designed to suit the requirements of the traditional colleges and universities. In the meanwhile, the schools preparing students through basic and post-basic education started disappearing. The Gandhian institutions which had supported the Rural Institutes declined in terms of their activities in the framework of Gandhi. Thus the Rural Institutes gradually lost their original character, mandate, approach and activities. They were all merged or affiliated with the traditional university system. The freedom of Gandhian experiments was given the go-by. The Rural Institutes started functioning as a soft variant of the traditional colleges and universities. Thus the Rural University or Rural Institute began to fade away. Only a few institutions have survived with lot of problems. Thus, the face of the rural university has been changed and it has assumed the characteristics of a college or a miniature traditional university.

New Initiatives

The concept of 'Rural University' gained much prominence after the release of the New Education Policy in the year 1986. It states that the new pattern of the rural university will be consolidated on the lines of Mahatma Gandhi's revolutionary ideas on education so as to take up the challenges of micro planning at the grassroots for the transformation of the rural areas for which institutions and programmes of Gandhian basic education will be supported. The policy envisages that educational institutions and voluntary agencies which take up educational programmes based on the concept of correlation between socially useful productive work, social service and academic study will be encouraged. Why did the New Education Policy reemphasize the need for the Rural Institute? It has to be viewed in perspective. Rural problems are mounting enormously and poverty reduction has become a real challenge to the rural development departments. Against this background the Central Government needed professional institutions to tackle the issues in the rural areas. Whether it was water supply, or sanitation, or livelihood, or primary education or primary health, or waste management, or rural energy, or rural employment the government required nodal institutions to help the government take appropriate policy decisions and implement them to achieve the targeted outcome. For this they needed institutions. Against this background the New Education Policy emphasized the need for rural higher education institutions. A Programme of Action was drawn up by the Ministry entitled New Education Policy, 1986. It advocated:

(a) Consolidation of the existing rural universities;
(b) Reorganization of the Rural Institutes established as a part of schemes of rural higher education launched in the Second Five Year Plan;
(c) Encouraging other institutions to take up Rural Reconstruction;
(d) Strengthening Rural Development Educational Programmes in select institutions;
(e) Supporting the elementary, secondary and post basic institute based on 'Nai Talim';
(f) Strengthening the content of all these institutions with emphasis on science and technology; and
(g) Setting up of National Rural Institutes Council to manage the affairs of Rural Institutes and Rural Universities.

Nothing moved beyond preparation of documents for about six years. This New Education Policy was modified in 1992 and, subsequently, based on the new recommendations, the National Council for Rural Institutions (NCRI) was established in 1995 at

Hyderabad by the Government of India. It is a registered society fully funded by the Government of India.[5]

It is to be noted here that how the newly created NCRI was to function was underlined clearly in the inaugural speech of the then Prime Minister of India, P.V. Narasimha Rao, on 3rd December, 1995.[6] His whole argument was to contextualize the Rural Institutes: they have to create cadres to manage development programmes. The cadres coming out from Rural Institutes should not be job hunters but job creators. The Rural Universities have to act as catalysts to help the communities through ideas, knowledge, skills and technology. These institutions have to transform the unskilled individuals into skilled workers to meet the market needs. The village life situation has to be transformed by implementing the constructive programmes, the activities ranging from village sanitation, water supply, livelihood, literacy, skill upgradation, small industries, infrastructure, communication, credit system, Panchayats act. The gap between the higher level government and the people has to be narrowed down. The Central Government evolves excellent policies, schemes and programmes. It allocates plenty of resources for rural development activities but they do not reach the field. The schemes and programmes evolved by the Central Government have to be implemented speedily and professionally for which the Rural Universities have to work continuously as facilitators. Appropriate technologies have to be developed in the Rural Institutes and they are to be disseminated and transferred to the communities. In China, two universities are helping rural artisans to prepare articles out of bamboo for export. In this way traditional universities are working in China to help the rural communities. The existing Rural Institutes in India have to rise to that level to lend their help to the rural community based on their experience. To evolve new technologies and to upgrade the skills needed by the market are the imperative tasks of the Rural Institutes. In this manner it was emphatically stressed, the Rural Institutes are to be contextualized[7] in the market era.

The Rural Institutes have to act as a support base for rural communities to make use of the opportunities coming from economic globalization and, at the same time, if threats issue from globalization, they are to be tackled by the community through the new Panchayati Raj System. Such a kind of contextualization has to be done in all Rural Universities.[8] Communities have to be in touch with the Rural Institutes for their needs. Such an interface has to be created between the Rural Institutes and the communities. A new cadre has to be created to manage the rural development programmes. These Rural Institutes are to be integrated with the larger society by which needed skills, capacity, technology and idea input will be provided. It was with this vision that the NCRI was created and, through a few Rural Universities was expected to function vibrantly. But now the question is how are they functioning and what have they achieved? These questions have to be answered objectively and honestly.

Assessment of the Second Phase

It is necessary to assess to what extent the second attempt to establish Rural Institutes and Universities has taken shape and to what extent the old Rural Institutes have lived up to their objectives. To be very frank, Rural Institutes were started but they could not survive and they disappeared. Only a few institutes are surviving. The NCRI was created only to rejuvenate the existing institutions and to establish new ones too. Hence, the assessment has to cover the NCRI and the old Rural Institutes surviving until now. First, one has to understand that rural development activities are facilitated not only by the Rural Institutes but also by many agencies in this country. There are government training institutions, specialized research institutes of higher order, departments (e.g. Rural Development) in traditional universities, civil society organizations continuously working for rural development by training the stakeholders involved in rural development activities, both leaders and officials, preparing needed cadres for rural development, assisting field work or working as outsourcing units. They are not designated as rural academic bodies but they do work for rural transformation and rural reconstruction.

Even after sixty years of continuous rural development activities by several agencies with plenty of schemes and programmes and pumping of huge resources, we could not make a bold statement that conditions have been created in the rural areas to facilitate a decent human life with all basic facilities. It is self-evident from the point of view of human development. Despite our schemes, programmes and huge resources for rural development, we could not create much impact on human development. Where are we now, in the human development report? Our position in human development will reveal our real achievements and failures. Even smaller countries with less growth have gone up in human development. Ours is a huge country with vast differences and it has been managed centrally and not in a decentralised fashion. Till now we have developed a perception among the people that 'development' is the work of the government and not of the community. People have developed a dependency syndrome and consider and perceived themselves as beneficiaries and petitioners, not as development participants or citizens. To tackle all the problems of the people in the rural areas, Governments both Central and State, develop plans centrally and not in a decentralised way. But it is an irony that some of our districts are larger than some countries in the world. Even within a state one finds a vast difference between or among the districts. Even within a district one finds much difference among the blocks. Genuine and effective decisions are taken, programmes are evolved, but to operationalise the same in different regions and sub-regions, concrete action plans are needed locally. Generic decisions, policies, programmes and schemes are chalked out but to dovetail them to the specific area, we need a specific action framework for implementation. Who will create such a plan at the district level and sub-district levels? The 74th Amendment to the Constitution of India says that it is mandatory on the part of every District Planning Committee to prepare a development plan for the whole of the district. But there is no district plan machinery barring in a few states.

India has got a vast human resource but they are not being used profitably. In the era of globalization, for global products, markets are found even in remote villages. But to find a market for local products, there is no integrated system. As a result, cottage and village industries are ruined. Many traditional skills have disappeared. Village life is not self-reliant but is dependent. In this way villages have been transformed. In fact, villages have been deserted. All economic activities are city and town centric. Hence one finds large scale migration from villages to urban areas and urbanization becomes rapid by the day. Economic growth has picked up. But living conditions in the rural areas are becoming difficult. The majority in the villages are living in sub-human living conditions. These are the reasons for our stagnation in the Human Development Index.

Three centuries ago India and China retained half of the wealth and riches in the world with half of the population in the world[9]. Now India, though poised for 8 to 9 per cent growth, cannot proclaim that it has enabled the people to lead a decent and dignified human life. Yet 71 per cent of the population is living in the rural areas. Of them 58 per cent to 60 per cent rely on agriculture for their livelihood.

Agriculture does not contribute substantially to economic growth and farmers have committed suicide due to crop failures due to the vagaries of the monsoon. The resulting large scale exodus of people to urban areas has made life in towns and cities miserable. The water level has gone down. Sanitation is poor in rural areas. Public schools have poor facilities and show ineffective functioning. Environmental degradation has set in. Skills in the rural areas have disappeared as they are not in demand. People have been reduced to beneficiaries and consumers rather than development participants. Still villages are in a feudal set-up as an agri-based economy is practiced and a hierarchical caste system plays a predominant role alongside patriarchy.

To bring about the needed change in the rural areas everyone looks to educational institutions. Why do we look to educational institutions for rural transformation despite the plethora of government programmes for rural development? For establishing effective linkage between the government and the communities we need catalyst institutions. The rural institutions can function as catalyst institutions. It does not mean that there are no higher educational institutions in the rural areas. There are many institutions in the rural areas but they are prototype Engineering Colleges, Arts and Science Colleges, Paramedical Training Institutions and even Medical Colleges. They are all just located in the rural areas. But there is absolutely no connection between the community and the educational institutions. Very near to the engineering colleges, villages are affected due to inadequate water supply and poor sanitation. This is not being attended to. It could be solved very easily by the intervention of the engineering colleges. Very near to medical colleges poor women and children are affected by anaemia and malnutrition. They could be attended to by the medical colleges. In reality they are not doing so. These educational institutions are modelled on the colonial pattern, which always commanded the intellectual resources of the people and never sought to educate the natives and draw out the best from them. The system excludes Dalits, women and tribals. Further the structure of these educational institutions has not been democratized, but remain hierarchical, nurturing the feudal culture. They are not only feudal and exploitative but also patriarchal. The staff are career oriented. They do not connect themselves with the society in the absence of a mandate for outreach programmes. By overcoming all these problems, educational institutions have to be reorganized to meet the requirements of the community. It is to be recognized and understood that the educational institutions have a rich potential to be extended to the community. But, unfortunately, we do not have an institutional mechanism to transfer the rich potential or extendables in the form of ideas, technologies and skills to the rural communities. Before the introduction of new Rural Institutes, the existing educational institutions have to find a way to reach out to the communities.

In each and every college, a department can be created for outreach programmes as a special drive of the University Grants Commission, by which systematic steps can be taken to conduct outreach programmes in the communities very near to a college or university. By doing so many of the issues and problems can be investigated by the academic institutions and, based on the findings, policy advocacy can be done by the same institutions. By doing all these activities, universities and colleges can establish effective linkages with the society. Thus even the traditional and conventional colleges and universities can reach out to the society systematically through an institutional mechanism. Then one can think about the establishment of Rural Institutes and Rural Universities.

Before planning the structure of the proposed new Rural Institutes, one has to analyse the functioning of the rural Institutions and the National Council for Rural Institutes. Before coming to evaluate the performance of the Rural Institutes one has to understand the reasons for many Rural Institutes merging with the traditional universities. The Rural Institutes were asked to work against the course of history. The direction of the Rural Institutes was quite opposite to the direction in which humanity moved.

The Rural Institutes were brought under the administrative system of the UGC, which is meant for conventional universities. The Rural Institutes which are in the ambit of the UGC have to move in the direction shown by the UGC. The leaders who are coming there for three years as Vice-Chancellors want to follow the guidelines of the UGC as it is the main funding agency instead of moving as per the objectives of the Rural Institutes. It is necessary that to manage the Rural Institutes, we identify persons with a deep understanding of the functioning of the Rural Institutes. But in reality, on many occasions, we cannot find persons with such a background to lead the Rural Institutes. Further the fundamental principles that shaped the edifice of the Rural Institute, the Gandhian framework, is yet another issue to be discussed. The whole Rural Institute concept is developed on the concept of "Nai Talim" of Gandhiji. The Rural Institutes came into being to cater to the needs of the students coming out from basic and post-basic education schemes. This amounted to developing a scheme of academic, research and extension activities on the principles of basic and post-basic education strongly rooted in 'Nai Talim' of Gandhiji. When basic and post-basic education were given a go-by how could Rural Institutes get students with such a background?

It is mandatory for the Rural Institutes to prepare the people for self-rule and build the capacity of the people to participate in the development process. But the development framework enunciated by Gandhiji has to be followed. The Rural Institutes have been brought under the framework of institutions which are in the process of modernization and industrialization. Having realized the weakness of this move, the National Council for Rural Institutes was created to set right the Rural Institutes. But the Rural Institutes were not brought under the domain of the NCRI. Thus NCRI became an entity like the ICSSR, the ICHR and other institutions to provide funding support to the institutes working on the objectives and programmes of the funding agencies. Though the NCRI was initially under the guidance of Dr. Aram, former Vice-Chancellor of Gandhigram Rural University, and later of Mr. L.C. Jain, a noted Gandhian, the NCRI was not placed on a sound ideological and financial footing. Both of them were highly respected Gandhians and recognized persons in the policy making bodies. When they were in the NCRI they were close to the government also. They could have impressed upon the policy makers the need of strengthening of the NCRI and bringing the Rural Institutes under the ambit of the NCRI. Both of them struggled with the bureaucrats even for the normal functioning of the NCRI. As a result the NCRI emerged as a funding agency to sponsor some of the activities of the institutions which are well within the Gandhian framework of activities. That is why the officials are asking why we need the NCRI to fund educational institutions and NGOs as we have the UGC and the Rural Development Ministry to fund these institutions respectively. We could not create a set of institutions which are well within the framework of the NCRI.

The Central Government has declarated that it would create world class management institutes, technology institutes, science institutes, central universities and so on. There is no mention about world class Rural Institutes to prepare cadres for rural development activities. Policy makers concentrate more on economic growth and human resource development in cities and towns and forget about the well-being of the people who are in the rural areas. Rural reconstruction and rural transformation need a totally different governance system, administrative system, livelihood system, economic system, credit system for which a new set of cadres are needed. An active interaction is needed between the academy and the communities. Gandhiji framed an ideal village system and this will be a referral point. This ideal village system has its own value framework. Keeping this in mind, the university has to work for it. One should not assume that the interaction between the institute and the community is free. There is the state, which takes up the responsibility of bringing development to the community. It takes decisions, evolves policies, prepares plans and allocates resources for all development activities. Yet development cannot be achieved. To achieve development, a catalyst action has to be performed by the Rural Institute. The New Panchayati Rai System has been established for which local body leaders and functionaries have to be trained and they are to be supported. As per the requirements of the Constitution of India, every district has to develop a development plan with the active participation of the people. For the preparation of the district plan, a planning machinery and a support structure are necessary. All development schemes require awareness among the people for implementation. The needed awareness has to be created. The available rural skills have to be enhanced. The skills have to be linked productively with the market system. A new support system is needed for farmers to come out from the present crises. A strong emphasis on research and development is required to support SHGs and village and cottage industries. Having said the contextual problems before contextualizing the whole framework of Rural University one has to bring to light what is exactly the Rural Institute or Rural University.

Rural University Framework

To get clarity on the concept of Rural University, one can go through the experience of the Visva Bharati University at Shantiniketan. Dr. Ramachandran had explained the experience with adequate clarity.[10] It is not a mere transplantation of city education in a rural area. It is a deeper process of a synthesis of the rural background with the challenges of modern society. Visva Bharati University demonstrated the very natural ambience with simplicity and scientific living conditions along with artistic beauty. Students will be able to understand the beauty of nature and the rhythm and cadences of nature with human interactions only when they are allowed to live with nature. Students will have opportunity to go deeper into the nature and its dimensions in relation to human interaction. Tagore emphasized the great values of Truth, Beauty and Goodness embedded in the ancient rural culture. This hoary past has to be rediscovered and the values have to be renourished as part of the activities of a Rural University. Though he emphasized the rediscovery of the old values of the rural culture of India, he equally emphatically and assiduously argued in favour of synthesis between the good values of the old rural culture of India with the values of modern civilization. The dominant thought that prevailed among the intellectuals, policy makers and policy makers was in favour of the system which was introduced by the British Administration in India. Even at the dawn of independence our leaders did not have the courage to introduce or to support the indigenous system of education. Even the intellectuals did not have the requisite argument to support the new system. It is only the Gandhian Scholars lamented on the theme and did conduct some experiments. To portray the characteristics of a Rural University I rely on the observations of Dr. G. Ramachandran as he was instrumental in establishing Gandhigram Rural Institute. Being a Gandhian Scholar and a student of Ravindra Nath Tagore his observations about Rural University are basic and authentic.

Rural University should be founded on an ideology that establishes conviction on the assumption that there are certain materials, mental and spiritual values in the ancient rural civilization and culture of India. The above values are to be discovered and renourished. It is to be made clear that this process do not contradicts the modern scientific and technological development values of the present day. One should understand the roots of the rural culture where one will find peacefulness as there was no competition for profit making exercise of individuals. The whole process of development is on cooperation for collective life either at the family life or at the community life. Cooperation adjustment, tolerances were with the attitude of the people in the rural areas.

Rural life is rooted in decentralization of political and economic power and resources with the aim of reaching out to the maximum of people. In the whole process of rural development one will find deeper and functioning of artistry in the life of the people in the rural commodities. One should take note here that in the name of ruralising higher education it never reflects adoption of scientific and technological values in rural human life.

Rural University takes higher education to the doorsteps of the people where they live closer to their occupation. The rural higher education is through the occupation of the people. It never keeps the people away from their occupation. It works on the improvement of the occupation through adoption of modern technology and scientific devices. Agriculture was the main basis of their occupation and hence the system of education is on agriculture primarily.

Further the Rural Higher Education touches upon the allied activities of agriculture in the rural areas. They are village industries and handicrafts. It is woven around village industries and handicrafts. It should be not a big one as the urban centric university system. It should be optimism in size but its reach has to be extensive through the outreach programmes. Extension methods play crucial roles in this university system.

Rural University should be in a position to rely on own resource both human and material. Teachers and students should be engaged in production activities. Rural University will follow two language formulas. One is mother tongue or regional language and Hindi, the national language. Any other language like English can be added. There should not be any subtraction from the two. Rural University unequivocally made it clear that it relies on local culture, practices, values and so on. India being culturally and spiritually rich and hence variations and diversities are abundant. Hence they are to be accommodated. While producing students from Rural University, it strives to produce men and women as not as products to the market as job seekers. But men and women will be prepared through proper orientation as an integrated personality to act as best citizens for the future. While orienting the students, the best spiritual traditions will be used. Rural University must revitalize the whole rural area where it is situated. Rural University campus will reflect the real transformation that takes place in the rural areas where the institute is located. Here one should register that even before the government took initiatives there experiments done by the Non-Governmental Organizations. Whether they are recognized or not, they were also useful experiments. Having seen the characteristics of a Rural University one has to consider the new Rural University in the context of Globalization.

Contextualization

The whole exercise has to be done in the backdrop of Globalization and the existing social and economic realities of rural India. The rural India has to be prepared to work towards social transformation by taking the advantages of globalization and decentralization and by avoiding the threats emanate from globalization and decentralization. Globalization has brought newer technologies and free flow of resources. They can be profitably used by the rural masses for their advantages. The existing problems in the rural areas have to be tackled. The problems are: livelihood of the poor, production of the agricultural sector, poor maintenance of commons, large scale migration, poor health of the women and children, poor sanitation, poor water supply, poor conditions for primary schools, energy crisis. Apart from the above rural governance is yet another issue to be looked after.

Primarily World Class University with potential staff can address the above issues through the academic, research and outreach programmes. It has to produce a cadre of outstanding individuals from the new rural universities not to seek jobs but to create jobs and manage development in the rural areas. Since Indian society has rich tradition, culture and civilization it should have a strong knowledge base. Hence they are to be explored, investigated. The new university has to work on the challenges of the rural society. By designing curriculum, offering programmes carrying out research all should be socially relevant. Rural University should be in policy advocacy front. In the same way it has to prepare qualified staff to rural development sector. It has to find out alternative approach of rural development which is sustainable in nature. It does not mean that it avoids globalization opportunities. It makes use of globalization opportunities and at the same time it avoids threats of globalization.[11] Now Nalanda University is in the formative stage which is going to concentrate on eastern knowledge.[12] It is to be noted that there is a general argument in India that educational system in India has not been concretely erected on Indian needs and ethos, which has ultimately affected the whole fabric of the Indian society.[13] In this context, the proposed Nalanda University and the Rural Universities will be of immense use to evolve a meaningful system of education in line with culture and ethos of India.

It should have a slim structure and delivery point should be broader. It need not follow the existing pattern of traditional Universities. It has to extend R&D support to all rural development activities. Be itself-help group or Agriculture or small scale industries or sanitation or water supply or traditional health practices or waste management, natural resource management, or energy from alternative source, or upgradation of rural skills, or enhancement of rural technology or rural governance or micro level planning, all can get the needed support from the Rural University. The new rural university will not be in comfort zone but it will be working on the challenges thrown by the rural communities. It not only creates cadres for rural development it will also train, orient the existing staff of rural development departments. Further it will build the capacity of the elected representatives of the local bodies. It will have effective linkage with rural communities, rural organizations and institutions. It should emerge as support institution for the rural communities and the government for effective management of rural development programmes. The new rural university will have a social audit system for its functions. Its impact on the society will be evaluated every five year by fixing certain observable indictors. The existing rural universities can be taken away from the UGC and put it under the NCRI. The funds have to be routed through the NCRI. The rural institutes need not follow the conventional Universities. It can develop its own pattern as the Indian Institute of Management, Ahmedabad.

Conclusion

'Rural University' has its own history in India since 1948. Yet concretely one cannot say that the Rural University has emerged as a matured educational system in India. Ever since it was recognized as a system of education in India from the dawn of independence it had been conceptualized yet government had not fully committed to extend support to this system. In all the times government provided only lip service and not extended full-fledged committed support. All the experiments have been faulted. Even the remaining institutions have changed this character. Thus a new rural university system has to be established to respond to the challenges of the rural society. The new rural university is need based, contextual, outreach and advocacy oriented. The new system should have manageable structure and delivery points extensive. Social audit system will be in place in the new rural university system.

Notes and References

1. K.C.R. Raja (ed.) *Thoughts and Talks of G. Ramachandran*, Gandhigram: Gandhigram Publications, 1964, pp. 310-312.
2. In the Communication of Government of India, Ministry of Education, No. 55-5/47-3/3 dated 4th November, 1948, there was no mention of rural university, but in the Section (IX) in terms of reference, there was a mention of the need for more universities on a regional or other bases. Taking the cue from the above, a separate section was written.
3. Since Rural India had its own livelihood, culture, trade, skills, crafts and so on for 80 per cent of the population, the author of the chapter in the Radhakrishnan Commission wanted to bring about transformation and reconstruction keeping the core values of India in focus and for this he suggested a new framework of education for rural development. Further the whole edifice of the framework has to be anchored on the concept of 'Nai Talim'. As per this chapter, the expansion of higher education should have been on this framework. But, unfortunately, it did not take place. Later there were different versions of the need for Rural Universities. One set of arguments is that it has to educate the rural masses formally and informally. Another set of arguments is that this university has to have live linkages with communities. It has to conduct outreach programmes. Yet another argument is projected about the role of rural university: it has to extend ideas, information, technology, skill, capacity and so on, to the rural communities through its outreach programmes and students learn by doing such activities. There is one more argument that it has to do research on rural development issues and help the community and the government to achieve the target of their activities.
4. Arun Kumar Dave, "A Rural University—Need of the Nation", *Ailaan* Vol. II: No. 11 (February, 2009).
5. National Council of Rural Institute, *A New Dawn on Rural Higher Education from Chaos to Order.* Hyderabad: National Council of Rural Institutes, 2001.
6. P.V. Narasimha Rao, "*Rural Universities: My Vision*". Inaugural Address. Hyderabad: National Council of Rural Institutes, 1995.
7. Ram Takwale, "Nai Talim of Connected Society with Education for Transformation", *Ailaan* Vol. II: No. 1 (January, 2009).
8. With the support of the Ford Foundation, serious studies have been conducted on the implications of globalisation and as a result a newsletter is being circulated among the Panchayats entitled '*Global and Local*'.

9. World Bank, *Reshaping Economic Geography: World Development Report,* 2009. Washington, DC: The World Bank, 2009.
10. Dr. G. Ramachandran had explained in one of his lectures the characteristics of a Rural University for more details refer Part Four, Seventh Chapter in K.C.R. Raja (ed.) *Thoughts and Talks of G. Ramachandran.* Gandhigram: Gandhigram Publications, 1964, pp. 310-317.
11. Gandhigram Rural Institute has prepared a blue print for making it as a Central Rural University and it is being submitted to the Government of India. For more details see Gandhigram Rural University, *Proposal for Gandhigram Central Rural University*. Gandhigram: University Publication, 2006.
12. S.D. Muni, "Nalanda: a soft power project", *The Hindu*, 31st August, 2010.
13. K.N. Panikkar, "Towards a New Paradigms in Education" *The Hindu* (9 May, 2009), p. 12.

Conclusion

Higher education in India is in an expansion mode. To the need of the market manpower has to be produced from the higher learning institutions. To produce the requirements of the market, number of higher learning institutions has to be increased. But the governments have not increased the resource allocation for such a massive expansion but it created an opportunity for the private to enter into higher education sector. As a result private individuals have started organizing higher learning institutions by making use of new opportunities created by the government. The regulatory institutions had to regulate the higher learning institutions through the framework which they have established. But there was no such rigorous regulatory process in place to maintain standard. As a result we find total mess, confusion, and exploitation in higher education system.

One cannot find immediate solution for the existing ills in our higher education system. The crisis we face in higher education is not material in nature. It is more of a moral crisis. It is not only with the institutions. It pervades everywhere. The whole macro system is afflicted with corruption. Education system is a sub-system of the macro system and hence it cannot escape from the main disease which afflicted the entire society. The governance leaders, whether they are Ministers of the Federal Government or Ministers of the State Government or Heads of various regulatory authorities at the federal and state levels have lost their moral authorities in the recent years as we have been seeing in the media day in and day out. Even the positions of Chancellors, Vice-Chancellors and Pro-Chancellors were once considered as moral authorities and they had moral statures but now they have lost the moral stature.

Opinion makers and the media took the lapses in education sector very seriously as it would affect the society in the long run. Destinies of the society are decided only by the knowledge institutions. Hence they make noise and voice. It is to be noted here that there is no strong action against this ill. But even the opinion makers are not seriously concerned about the deterioration of the higher education system. The teachers over a period of time expressed their concern about the issues of the society apart from fighting for their own benefits. Now they have also not shown any concern for the fall of the higher education system in India. Absolutely they have abdicated their roles and responsibilities. Since teachers have not evinced interest and concern for the issues, the students have not been oriented to be conscious on the issues of the society and even on the issues affecting their life also.

At this point of time by assessing the existing conditions of the higher learning institutions private players have entered into the higher education domain and they contributed both positively and negatively for the expansion of higher education system in India. While criticizing the existing conditions of higher education in India foreign universities are also coming to India to serve us. It is being visualized both positively and negatively. *In toto*, the system is not able to produce the quality manpower needed to the job market. At the same time it could not cater to the needs of the people also. Moreover the cost of education is very high and the whole higher education system has come to exploit the society without much interference and control of the regulatory bodies of the government. Where is the solution? is the question. The present book tries to give answer to the above question. Solution lies in many domains.

First, the subject 'education' should go either to Central list or State list. Now it is in Concurrent list. It helps only to add confusion and not to bring clarity. Many of the state governments are posing demands to the Central Government to transfer the subject from concurrent list to state list as it was before emergency. In the new context we need a new policy as globalization has unleashed its power. Regulatory bodies have to be created with moral authority. The image of regulatory authorities has to be enhanced. Persons with moral stature have to be appointed as head of the regulatory authorities. Even with regard to the appointment of Vice-Chancellors, enough care has to be taken to bring more stature to the positions by appointing reputed scientists and intellectuals as Vice-Chancellors. Higher learning institutions have to be equipped in terms of the facilities. Then only they can deliver goods effectively. Yet, to start with, teachers have to play a crucial role by performing their roles and responsibilities with the sense of commitment and professionalism. In this book through all the articles much emphasis was given for the missing role of the teachers in Universities—'Extension'. The author brings to light the neglected and missing role of the outreach activities of the teachers. Teachers have multidimensional roles in Colleges and Universities. They are teaching, research and extension. By doing all the roles many of the issues of the society will be tackled effectively and professionally. Teachers have to take up socially relevant issues for research and the research findings have to be taken up for policy advocacy. The teachers have to generate opinion on all public issues based on facts and research findings.

Further socially conscious and socially sensitive students have to be prepared for social action and quality research. Higher educational institution should earn the name and reputations from the public and the government. In such a way the institutions have to perform. A new quality culture has to be created to change the mindset of the policy makers and the public. By doing the conscious work in the higher learning institutions by the teacher, the existing scenario can be changed. Hence works and initiatives have to be started from the teachers and the institutions. A new culture has to be created in the higher learning institutions.

Bibliography

Agarwal Pawan, "From Kothari Commission to Pitroda Commission", *Economic and Political Weekly,* February 17, 2007.

Anandakrishnan, M., "Critique of Knowledge Commission", *Economic and Political Weekly,* February 17, 2007.

Ananta Kumar Giri, (ed.) *Rethinking Social Transformation.* New Delhi: Rawat Publications, 2001.

Balleisen, Edward J. and Moss, David A. (eds.), *Government and Markets: Towards a New Theory of Regulation,* Cambridge: Cambridge University Press, 2010.

Baumgartner Ruedi and Hogger Ruedi, (eds.) *In Search of Sustainable Livelihood Systems Managing Resources and Change,* New Delhi: Sage Publications, 2004.

Cloke Paul, Terry Marsden and Partrick H. Mooney (eds.) *Handbook of Rural Studies,* New Delhi: Sage Publications, 2006.

Dr. S. Radhakrishnan's *University Education Commission* (1949), *Shrimali Committee* (1955), *Ramachandran's Committee* (1969) Reports.

Edward J. Balleisen and David A. Moss (eds.) *Government and Markets: Towards a New Theory of Regulation,* Cambridge: Cambridge University Press, 2010.

Epp Roger and Whitson Dave, (eds.) *Writing off the Rural West: Globalisation Governments and the Transformations of Rural Communities.* Edmonton: University of Alberta Press and Parkland Institute, 2001.

Gandhigram Rural University, *Proposal for Gandhigram Central Rural University.* Gandhigram: University Publication, 2006.

Gandhi, M.K., *Village Swaraj,* Ahmedabad: Navajeevan Trust, 1962.

Gupta, G.P. (ed.) *Management by Consciousness: A Spirituo-technical Approach.* Pondicherry: Sri Aurobindo Institute of Research in Social Sciences, 1994.

International Commission on Peace and Food, *Developing Human Resourcefulness.* California: International Commission on Peace and Food, 1989.

Joseph Thomas, "Commission versus Commission in Higher Education", *Economic and Political Weekly,* December 15, 2007.

Jugal Kishore Mukherjee, *Principles and Goals of Integral Education.* Pondicherry: Sri Aurobindo Ashram, Publication Department, 2005.

Kishowar Madhu Purnima, *Deepening Democracy: Challenges of Governance and Globalisation in India,* New Delhi: Oxford University Press, 2005.

Kumar Dave Arun, "A Rural University—Need of the Nation", *Ailaan* Vol. II: No. 11 (February 2009).

Ministry of Human Resource Development, *Report of the Committee to Advise on Renovation and Rejuvenation of Higher Education,* New Delhi: Government of India, 2009.

Muni, S.D., 'Nalanda: A soft power project', *The Hindu,* 31st August, 2010.

Mohanty, Ranjita and Tandon, Rajesh (eds.) *Participatory Citizenship: Identity, Exclusion and Inclusion,* New Delhi: Sage Publications, 2006.

National Council of Rural Institute, *A New Dawn on Rural Higher Education from Chaos to Order,* Hyderabad: National Council of Rural Institutes, 2001.

National Knowledge Commission: *Report to the Nation 2006;* UGC, *A Brief Report of the National Conference on Development of Higher Education,* October 10-11, 2007; and *Report of the Commission to Advise on Renovation and Rejuvenation of Higher Education,* 2009.

National Knowledge Commission, *National Knowledge Commission: Report of The Nation* 2006, New Delhi: Government of India, 2006; University Grants Commission, *A Brief Report of The National Conference on Development of Higher Education,* New Delhi: University Grants Commission, 2007; MHRD, *Report of The Commission to Advise on Renovation and Rejuvenation of Higher Education,* New Delhi, Government of India, 2009.

Panikkar, K.N., "Towards a New Paradigm in Education", *The Hindu* (9 May, 2009).

Palanithurai, G. "Higher Education in India: Where are we leading", *University News,* Vol. 48: No. 28, July 12-18, 2010.

Palanithurai, G., "Rural Universities in the era of Globalization", *University News,* Vol. 47: No. 33 (August, 2009); G. Planithurai, "Larger Role of Academics in Rural Human Life", *University News,* Vol. 47: No. 16, (April 2009).

Palanithurai, G., "Governance and Administration Reform at Grassroots" *Public Administration,* Vol. 4: No. 4 (Oct., 2008)

Palanithurai, G. and Ramesh, R., *Globalisation and Decentralisation,* New Delhi: Concept Publishing Company Pvt. Ltd., 2008.

Palanithurai, G., R. Ramesh, *Actionable Learning Handbook for Local Self-Government,* Rajiv Gandhi Chair for Panchayati Raj Studies, 2007.

Palanithurai, G., *Globalization: Concerns at the grassroots and how to address them?* Gandhigram: Rajiv Gandhi Chair for Panchayati Raj Studies, 2007.

Palanithurai, G., *Managing Globalization—A Guidebook for Panchayats,* Gandhigram: Rajiv Gandhi Chair for Panchayati Raj Studies, 2008.

Palanithurai, G., *Report of the National Workshop for Validating the Research Studies on Globalization and Decentralization* Gandhigram: Rajiv Gandhi Chair for Panchayati Raj Studies, 2007.

Peter, G. Northouse, *Leadership: Theory and Practice,* New Delhi: Sage Publications India Private Limited, 2007.

Ramachandran, R., "University Business", *Frontline,* July 17, 2009.

Ramachandran, R., "It has to be a Constitutional Body: Interview with Yash Pal", *Frontline,* July 17, 2009.

Ramesh K. Arora and Meena Sogani (eds.) *Governance in India: Paradigms and Practices.* Jaipur: Aalekh Publishers, 2010.

Rao Narasimha, P.V., "*Rural Universities: My Vision*". Inaugural Address. Hyderabad: National Council of Rural Institutes, 1995.

Rajalakshmi, T.K., "The Increase Explained: Interview with S.K. Thorat UGC Chairperson", *Frontline* July 17, 2009.

Raja, K.C.R. (ed.) *Thoughts and Talks of G. Ramachandran.* Gandhigram: Gandhigram Publications, 1964.

Salmi, J., *Tertiary Education in the 21st Century: Challenges and Opportunities,* Washington DC: World Bank, 2000.

Stella Anthony and Gnanam, A., *Looking Ahead: A Decade of Accreditation in Retrospect: Development in Quality Assurance of Higher Education in India,* Bangalore: Aicra Publishers, 2004.

Shah, Beena, "Indian Higher Education: New Horizons and Plausible Challenges ...whilting a way Ahead", *University News,* Vol. 48: No. 28, July 12-18, 2010.

Sharma, Ravi, "Main Markets", *Frontline*, July 17, 2009.

Sonalde, Desai and Veena Kulkarni, "Changing Educational Inequalities in India in the context of Alternative Action" *Demography,* Vol. 45: No. 2, May, 2008.

Stiglitz, Joseph, *Globalisation and its Discontents*, New Delhi: Penguin Books, 2003.

Stiglitz, Joseph, *Making Globalisation Works.* New York: Allen Lane, 2006.

Sibal, Kapil, Minister for Human Resource Development made a commitment that Structural Reform will be within 100 days.

Takwale, Ram, "Nai Talim of Connected Society with Education for Transformation", *Ailaan* Vol. II: No. 1 (January 2009).

UNESCO, "*Learning: The Treasure Within" Report To UNESCO of The International Commission on Education for Twenty First Century*, Paris: UNESCO, 1996.

Viswanathan, S., "Tamil Nadu", *Frontline*, July 17, 2009.

World Bank, *Reshaping Economic Geography: World Development Report,* 2009. Washington, DC: The World Bank, 2009.

Index